MW00638405

"HollyKem and Dean a
to the field of recovery.
audiences and now are extending their repertoire of
information to reach people through an exciting
book—*A Roadmap to the Soul.* We believe everyone can
find a life direction—here is a new tool to assist on
your journey. Enjoy!"

Marvel Harrison Kellogg, Ph.D. and Terry Kellogg, M.A.

* * * * * *

"Original, inspiring, a great vocabulary for healing
and recovery."

Johnny Rainer, Director
Jolimar Summit Wellness Institute

* * * * * *

"*A Roadmap to the Soul* is a unique and engaging ap-
proach to wellness and the development of the 'Whole
Person.' While it is written as a self-help book, one
immediately recognizes its value for parents who are
seeking ways to encourage their children to develop a
positive self-concept. The authors' extensive use of
metaphors such as the 'protector' and 'true self' provide a rich array of language that can be used to
communicate the key concepts of mental wellness in a
manner that pre-teens through adults can understand."

James Duplass, Professor of Education
The University of South Florida

* * * * * *

"I live a soulful life because of The Voices Within
concept that HollyKem and Dean have outlined in
these pages. It has been a great blessing."

Barbara M., a recovering addict/alcoholic

A Roadmap to the Soul

A Practical Guide to Love, Compassion, and Inner Peace

by HollyKem Sunseri, BCSAC
and
F. Dean Sunseri, MA, MED, LPC

TVW Publishing
Metairie, LA 70002

First printing 1999

ISBN 1-892128-62-4

LCCN 98-60846

Editing, design, typesetting, and printing services provided by About Books, Inc., 425 Cedar Street, POB 1500, Buena Vista, CO 81211, (800) 548-1876.

ATTENTION CORPORATIONS, UNIVERSITIES, COLLEGES, AND PROFESSIONAL HEALTH ORGANIZATIONS: Quantity discounts are available on bulk purchases of this book for educational purposes. Special books or book excerpts can also be created to fit specific needs. For information, please contact TVW Publishing, 3017 12th Street, Metairie, LA 70002, (504) 838-0486 or (888)889-7600. www.IHaveAVoice.com

CONTENTS

ACKNOWLEDGMENTS

We would like to thank our families for their love and support. Helen Rogers has been a constant help through this process, cooking, cleaning, praying and believing in us more than we believe in ourselves. Linda and Frank Sunseri have been a source of love and encouragement.

We would like to thank all of our friends, especially those in our support groups. Their constant nurturing and friendship provided us with energy to recharge our batteries. Thank you to all our clients; you have helped us understand the power of The Voices Within. Thank you Robert Hale, Richelle Aime, Tammie Chaplain, Marc D'Aunoy, and Ann Wilkerson for your friendship and hard work. Karen Cortello, and Sue Maksen–thank you for reading, editing, and giving us loving suggestions. Thank you Marilyn and Tom Ross and the supporting staff at About Books, Inc.

We thank our patron St. Jude for his intercession. Most of all we want to *thank God* for the gifts of abundant life, love, creativity, and inspiration.

Go Moses

Moses leading the people to Freedom

A long time ago, there was a baby found in a river by a princess. The princess adopted the baby and gave him the childhood of a prince. As the prince grew up, he knew he did not belong in the royal family. Eventually, he left his kingdom as a young man in search of his true identity. During his search for his true self, he realized his family was enslaved.

He continued his journey and he met his God on a mountain top. He found his purpose in life: *freedom*. He became a leader to free himself and his people. God gave him power, which was symbolized by a shepherd's staff. He met his oppressor, the Pharaoh, who did not want to let his people go. Moses worked great signs and wonders in Egypt, and his oppressor reluctantly granted them freedom.

Heading for the Promise Land, the oppressed people began to make the journey. Moses led the people to the desert. "You must journey through the desert before you reach the Promise Land," Moses told the people. The people wanted freedom, but some of them did not want to go through the desert. Moses was amazed some people preferred slavery to the journey to freedom. Some said, "I want to go back to Egypt where we have food, work, and security." Enslavement can be attractive compared to the hardship and loneliness of the desert. Others said, "Let's set up a home at an oasis in the desert." The temporary security of an oasis is safer than the uncertain journey ahead. Some of the people asserted, "I will embrace this journey in the desert until we get to the Promise Land, because God has brought us this far and He will not fail us now." Some people experienced the miracles that were worked in Egypt, yet they continued to doubt the power of God.

Moses led the people through the desert to the Promise Land. The Promise Land is a place of freedom where God and His people live in harmony. The journey of Moses and his people was an external journey. Our journey to the Promise Land of freedom and soulful living is an internal one. We must be willing to journey within. We will guide you with a roadmap that will result in love, compassion and inner peace.

Each one of us is called to make the journey from enslavement to freedom. We are challenged to face our oppressor and battle for power by aligning with our spiritual vision. Moses found his power through the symbol of the shepherd's staff and it gave him the ability to defeat the Pharaoh. We must find the shepherd's staff inside ourselves and learn to utilize this power to defeat our internal oppressors. We are asked to journey into the desert of emotional pain. Moses traveled through the desert with courage, faith and hope that better things are in the future. We need to embrace the desert of our emotional pain with courage, faith and hope that freedom and life await us on the other side. Each one of us is invited to enter into the Promise Land of the True Self and enjoy soulful living.

The Promise Land

To shine within, to love within,
To feel within, to trust within,
To listen within, and to be within.
To BE as a child would be,
FREE!
To have and express faith.
To shine like the Sun,
The light, the power, the warmth,
the brightness, the glow.
To love as a child loves.
To express my Pain and Joy as a child.
To forgive as a child.
This is Soulful Living
This is the Promise Land.

* * * * * *

The Voices Within is a language of love for self, others, and God. It is a roadmap to embrace oneself, others, and God while learning to be *free* in love, compassion and inner peace. If one embraces the Voices Within concept and uses it as a living tool, one can have everything.

The three voices inside the head.

The Voices Within

The Voices Within is a language to help you understand yourself. It is a simple concept that can serve as a doorway to freedom and peace. The basic idea is that the personality can be divided into three parts: one part is called the True Self. It is the soul, the passion, the creative spark that yearns for peace and embraces life. One part is the Wounded Child, which is the part that carries our internalized pain. The third part is the Protector, and this part is our coping mechanism. Does this mean there are three different personalities inside each one of us? No! It is simply a language that helps us understand why we do the things we do and why we feel the way we do.

The three most important relationships we have as human beings are those with ourselves, others, and God. All of these relationships influence each other tremendously. A man who has a terrible image of himself will have a difficult time relating to other people and God. The Voices Within is a roadmap to help one love oneself.

This self-acceptance is the foundation that will help you develop life-giving relationships with others and with God. All three levels of relating are extremely important; nevertheless, we will focus on the relationship with the self because this is the foundation. How can you love another person unless you have a self? How can you relate and love God unless you have a self? Our quest is to find the unique True Self in each person.

We call the different parts voices; they are in our heads and speak to us all day long. The messages are endless and continue from dusk to dawn. It can be overwhelming! If you stop and listen, you will hear the voices talking.

"Keep quiet, stupid!"

"Don't look in his eyes."

"I don't want to get out of bed."

"You need to get out of bed."

"Divorce is sinful."

"Yeah, well *she* never comes home at night."

For example, a man in a car approaches the stop light that just turned yellow. The voices are ringing inside the man's head and he must make a decision.

"Go for it! Push the gas!"

"Stop, idiot; you're going to get a ticket."

"Keep going slowly; it just turned yellow."

This book will help you categorize and understand these voices, as well as find the voice of your soul. What separates our treatment from many other theories is the Protector. There are many therapies that help you work with the voice of the Wounded Child, but they don't clearly make the connection between the wounds and the coping mechanism (Protector). When this bridge is made, many of our clients find a deep sense of self-understanding and self-forgiveness. Both the wound and the defense mechanism must be embraced to find permanent movement.

Throughout the journey of this book, you will be asked to do different exercises. The most important exercise will be for you to name your Protector and your Wounded Child. It is through naming, claiming, and loving these parts you will find contentment and freedom. Our goal in this process is not to *heal* your Wounded Child completely or to *get rid* of your Protector but to give you the skills to manage these voices on your own. You have the rest of your life to deal with them.

We are writing this book as a team. HollyKem is a board-certified Substance Abuse Counselor. She has worked as a primary therapist in a halfway house for women and in an in-patient treatment center; she has also worked as a private practitioner. Dean is a Licensed Professional Counselor with masters degrees in Mental Health Counseling and in Theology. We have been married for more than six years, and this book is an extension of that partnership. We make a good team because HollyKem's thinking is circular and Dean's is linear. We explain most of our concepts in these different ways, so both types of thinkers will understand.

For the maximum benefit, we suggest you read the content of the book and complete the exercises. We recommend you invest in an art pad and colored pens or paints and a notebook for journaling. Some of the exercises you can do right in the book; others you can do in your notebook and on your art pad.

The road to the Soul

CHAPTER 1

Journey to the Soul

Mental health counseling, therapy, and analysis are primarily twentieth-century inventions. Why do so many people spend time and effort in these endeavors? The reasons are endless not only for those receiving the service but also for those who give the service. Counseling, therapy, and analysis help people solve problems, release emotions, change negative thoughts, gain insight into oneself, relieve anxiety, relieve depression, and improve or deal with failed relationships. We must make the unconscious conscious, says the psychoanalyst, while the cognitive therapist claims we must change our thought patterns. The Gestalt counselor loves to release emotion, and Rogerians say the therapist must unconditionally accept the client. These are worthy goals, but what is the payoff? The reason we have so many different theories is that none of them provides a suitable answer to the spiritual nature of our humanity. They provide some relief, greater insight, and sometimes a more fulfilling life, but they do not feed the deeper yearnings of the human soul.

The greatest sin today is that people are out of touch with their souls. The soul, which is missing in action, is lost behind obsessive behaviors: the gambler zoned out behind the video poker machine; the retired salesman living in his recliner zoned out in front of the television. Then there is the woman shopping in the department store who is in a trance, detached from her spirit, and the crack addict whose eyes tell the story of a soul that has disappeared along with his or her conscience. Take a walk in the local mall and see all the people who are nothing more than zombies. Where has the invigorating human spirit gone? Life without the soul is impersonal, disconnected, and lonely. It is limited, inhibited, and suppressed behind a protected palace that is beyond reach. *The soul is lost!*

Discovering the soul is our deepest human yearning. If our life journey does not include this breakthrough, it will not satisfy. Emptiness and despair will accompany both the greatest accomplishments and the worst failures. Recovering the voice of our soul means we uncover our passion, our God, our connection to the world, and our purpose in life. It is a journey that requires a roadmap. There have been many successful roadmaps throughout the ages. In fact, religions are built around these successful roadmaps. Unfortunately, the roadmaps of yesterday may not work today. They need to be updated and transformed into today's language.

The Voices Within is a roadmap to the soul. It has successfully helped individuals to become alive, to find their passion and dreams, and to create a soulful existence. We invite you to use our roadmap to discover, uncover, and understand your soul more deeply.

There is one assumption in soulful work that has to do with the Maker of our soul–God. Our belief is that God created us, inside and out. On the exterior, God meets us in nature, rituals, religions, communities, and other places filled with the Spirit. On the interior, He meets us in our souls. Soulful work is impossible to accomplish without God. In your own process of recovering your soul, we suggest you ask God for help and guidance. If you do not have a relationship with God, ask for the willingness to believe. God is the healer of broken hearts, and without God there is no healing.

Human Condition

As a seminarian, Dean remembers talking to a monk one day about the spiritual crisis in today's world. He was a very simple and brilliant man who loved to work in his herb garden. Dean asked him, "Why do you think people have a difficult time being spiritual today?"

He told Dean the problem is not about being spiritual but about being human. "People do not know how to be human," he said. "We first must love our humanness before we can really understand our true relationship with God." At the time, Dean did not understand what he meant, but his comment made a deep impression.

We are created to be human, yet we often attempt to escape this condition. Part of the human condition is suffering. In an attempt to escape suffering, we often create more pain. If we don't know how to embrace our human condition, greater suffering results. We are told the following by others:

"Be perfect."

"Don't feel."

"Don't think."

"Don't be human."

We are supposed to shut off our feelings and simply *do*. When we become fat, addicted, codependent busybodies, other people criticize us. We must go back to the basics. *We must learn to be human*. We must learn to embrace ourselves and our suffering and to love ourselves. We know it can be done. HollyKem was a hopeless alcoholic and drug addict who thought she had lost everything. If she was able to learn to be human, so can you. Tell yourself, "I am a person who suffers and a person who trusts and loves today. I love myself!"

CHAPTER 2

HollyKem

I find myself—a thirty-seven-year-old woman—sitting in my country kitchen with a cup of coffee. I am finally in touch with my soul. It has taken many years of recovery to unearth my soul or as I call it, my True Self. The last fifteen years have been spent in twelve-step meetings and therapy and with caring friends and my mother. For the first time in my life I feel centered, whole, loving, and lovable, and I have something to contribute to the world. I remember attending a John Bradshaw workshop, and he said the greatest sin of all is to die without knowing yourself. This made a deep impression on me, and I decided it would not happen to me! The concept of the Voices Within is a description of my journey to discover my True Self.

"I Have a Voice" initially meant my Wounded Child has a voice. The part of me that carries my pain from the past finally has the safety and freedom to speak. I realized my Protector has had a voice for a long time. In twelve-step meetings, I discovered this voice. When I introduced myself, "Hi, I'm HollyKem; I am an addict/alcoholic," I was actually introducing my Protector. Through the process of understanding, loving, nurturing, and separating my Wounded Child and my Protector, the voice of my True Self emerged.

Dean

As a thirty-two-year-old man–make that a thirty-three-year-old man as I just had my birthday two days ago–I too am sitting in my country kitchen. I have recently become aware of the wonderful sensation of *feeling* like a man and *being* a man. I used to believe education was the solution to finding my manhood and my soul. After completing two masters degrees, I made honorable academic achievements, but I did not feel like a man. I felt more like a smart boy. Today, I can see how my education has given me many gifts, such as the ability to write this book, but it did not give me my manhood.

For many years, I wandered in search of my True Self. I was lost. My journey took me to Europe, the Middle East, Central America, Canada, and across the United States. I began to discover my Wounded Child during my seminary years with my spiritual advisor, Father William. His encouragement got me involved in twelve-step meetings where I began to discover my Protector. It finally dawned on me I would find my soul within myself. Finding the True Self is an inside job. Working with the Voices Within has given me the tools to find what I have been searching for. For the first time in my life, my True Self has a voice, and I love it.

I Have a Voice

What does "I Have a Voice" mean? Literally, it says one's beliefs have an expression and these beliefs are understood by oneself. It means one understands the three basic belief systems of one's Wounded Child, Protector, and True Self. Having a voice means having the power to choose the belief system upon which to act. For example, when one needs to go to work the Wounded Child may want to stay home in bed. The Protector may want to call in sick to obey the Wounded Child's wishes. The True Self (the adult) needs to go to work to support the family. Having a voice means having the power to make decisions that are healthy and not self-destructive.

Having a voice means having the ability to share one's entire self with another person intimately, personally, and completely. It allows one to communicate neediness, woundedness, and anger while still being an adult. For many years the only way HollyKem knew how to communicate her neediness, woundedness, anger, and pain was to *be it*. The tragedy is she could not separate these things from her True Self. Having the ability to separate means having the ability to love and to not be lonely.

CHAPTER 3

Possession of the Voices

Internal Possession

In the movie *Ghost*, Whoopi Goldberg plays a psychic who becomes possessed by spirits that have gone to the next world. When she is possessed by these spirits her body is no longer her own; she is at the mercy of whatever the spirit wants to say or do. Her voice and body language change, and she acts out of the belief system of the spirit. This is an excellent illustration of what happens when we are possessed by our woundedness or our coping mechanisms.

When Dean was teaching in high school, he got a note in his mailbox that the principal wanted to talk to him. Dean became instantly terrified. He felt like a small child being sent to the principal's office. He was *possessed*–a thirty-year-old man who suddenly felt like a six-year-old child. A voice told Dean to run and make up an excuse. "You need to avoid this meeting at all costs," the voice said loudly.

When Dean and HollyKem were dating, Dean went out of town one weekend. He had promised to call HollyKem on Friday night, but he forgot. HollyKem was *possessed.* One voice said Dean had left her. Another said he was with another woman. Another said he was dead. HollyKem felt abandoned and scared. Then another voice took over, saying, "Screw him! He's no good anyway. He doesn't make enough money, and he is too young." The inner conversation dominated HollyKem's being the entire night.

Enmeshment

Enmeshment is the inability to separate the voices and to separate the internal from the external. Many therapists call this a lack of boundaries. It makes it difficult to make a good decision. Internal enmeshment means the individual does not know the difference between the Protector, Wounded Child, and True Self. It is like a committee inside the head. All of these thoughts are racing at once; it is chaos, obsession, and pain, with no peace of mind. *Help!*

For example, here are Sam's thoughts: Sales are slow at work.

I'm going to get fired.

My kids are going to starve.

So what! I hate this job.

Everything is going to be okay.

No, the depression is returning.

My wife is going to divorce me.

Rhonda's thoughts: My kid is failing and I have an appointment with the teacher.

I'm going to kill that kid.

I'm a terrible mother.

I'm so embarrassed.

I need to get a tutor for my child.

I'm a total failure.

Can I hide this from his father?

Beth's thoughts: My husband is working late.

He is having an affair.

I'm too fat and ugly.

He has a lot of work to do.

He is at a bar drinking.

I won't have sex with him.

Ralph's thoughts: Honey, we can spend the entire weekend together.

She is trying to control me.

I'll get to spend time with my girlfriend.

She will smother me!

I'll lie and say I have plans—golf, work, baseball, any excuse.

How we eventually react to situations depends on which voice we listen to or which voice has the most power. When we don't know who is talking within, we are in a state of internal enmeshment/internal pain.

External enmeshment is being connected to other people's belief systems, and decision making is based on the thoughts and opinions of others. It is a childlike state where the locus of authority is with another person. The word "codependency" is commonly used to describe this external enmeshment. Examples include the woman who cannot make a decision without the approval of her husband. The man who chooses a profession based solely on financial success. The woman who marries a man because her father approves. The man who chooses not to have children because he doesn't want to repeat the cycle of addiction. These are all instances of external enmeshment.

When our woundedness or our protective mechanisms are relating to the world, our True Self is lost in the process. Loneliness is the result and it can mean different things. There is loneliness in a relationship or loneliness because one is not in a relationship, or in a family or because there is no family, or on the job or because there is no job. Loneliness is not the result of external circumstance, it is internal. Loneliness is the result of being possessed by the voices.

Many people often say to HollyKem they are lost and need to find themselves. She used to be puzzled by this because they were sitting in front of her talking. Then HollyKem began to realize these individuals related to the world through their Wounded Voice or their Protector Voice. Their True Self was indeed lost. Being possessed by the Wounded Voice or the Protector Voice is one of the great tragedies. It causes much pain, misunderstanding, suffering, and despair.

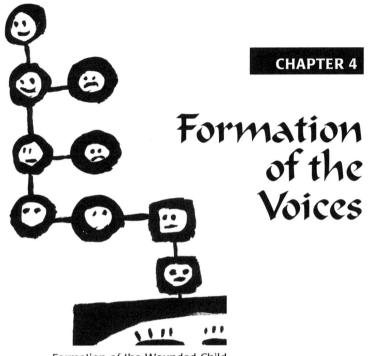

CHAPTER 4

Formation of the Voices

Formation of the Wounded Child
and the Protector

Formation

In the beginning we are born healthy. God gives us all the potential we need to become flourishing humans. Besides having basic physical needs met, the only other requirements we have are nurturing and love. We must be cared for emotionally, physically, intellectually, and spiritually. Because of human limitations, it is impossible to have these needs met perfectly. No family or parent is capable of providing for a child a perfectly safe and nurturing setting all the time.

In addition, part of the human condition means we will experience painful events. If we are in a safe and nurturing environment, we will heal from these experiences. If the en-

13

vironment is not safe in one or more areas, then we *internalize* the pain. Internalized pain is any uncomfortable feeling stored in the body. *Pain is an uncomfortable emotion.* Loneliness, sadness, anger, fear, depression, hopelessness, and hurt are just a few of the feelings we consider pain. Internalized pain is how our Wounded Child is created.

Imagine a six-year-old child whose parents are going through a divorce. Because the parents are in their own emotional pain about the divorce, the environment is not safe for the child to heal from the trauma. This child feels abandoned, lost, lonely, and scared. A child is naturally self-centered and believes the breakup in the family is about him or her. Because of the lack of safety, the child will *internalize* the pain rather than *externalize* his or her feelings. This experience will create a belief about marriage, about relationships, about relating to others, and about the child's image in the neighborhood. This is an example of how the belief system of the Wounded Child begins. It is caused by internalized pain. When this child becomes an adult, part of his or her belief system will continue to be based on the pain of the divorce.

Inner Child

There is an inner child inside each of us that is separated into two parts: the Magical Child and the Wounded Child. The Magical Child holds the good memories of happiness and love and is part of the True Self. The Wounded Child holds the painful memories of fear, abandonment, and loneliness. Individuals who have not embraced their woundedness often have memory loss of the past. Both the painful and the happy memories are gone, waiting to be recaptured. We cannot get to the Magical Child unless we go through and embrace our woundedness. We must do the one thing that was not done for the Wounded Child; we must *love it in its pain.*

Healthy and Unhealthy Families

Even in the healthiest families, each individual will store some pain and develop a Wounded Child. The storehouse of pain will naturally be much larger in an unhealthy family that does not know how to deal with emotional pain. It is natural for a family to experience losses such as death, sickness, addiction, and divorce. The test of health is how the family copes with the losses. It is known that to heal from a loss, each individual must go through the grief process. The stages of the grief process follow.

Stage	Feeling
Denial	Numbness
Anger	Anger, frustration, rage
Bargaining	Obsession, guilt, shame
Pain	Sadness, loneliness, hurt, hopelessness, depression
Acceptance	Freedom, forgiveness, relief

When a person goes through the grief process, he or she moves back and forth through different stages and feelings. Depending on the severity of the loss, the individual will stay in the grief process for a variable amount of time. A woman whose husband has recently died may stay in the grief process for three years, whereas a boy whose best friend has moved away may need to grieve for two months.

When a family experiences a loss, it is important to understand each individual in the family may be at a different stage at any given time. Healing movement happens when an individual is safe enough to move into denial, anger, bargaining, pain, and acceptance. We call this DABPA, which is an acronym for the different stages of the grief process. For example, a family that recently has lost a close relative will be in DABPA. The father is in anger, while the mother is in pain. One child is in denial and the other is in bargaining. Safety and love help each individual move toward acceptance.

On our honeymoon, we went to Greece where we noticed some of the women wearing black. Dean later found out a Greek woman wears black for up to a year after her husband dies. This is a wonderful ritual to help the woman grieve. The black is a symbol to the community that this woman is in pain and that she needs extra love and support. Our culture does not have good rituals to help us deal with pain. We are lucky to get a couple of days off of work when a loved one dies. Our culture fosters the development of the Wounded Child by encouraging us to internalize our pain.

As losses continue in an individual's life, a person must learn how to deal with his or her pain. If the environment is not safe, the individual will hold it inside and the Wounded Child will grow. As the Wounded Child grows, it becomes bigger than the Magical Child. Spontaneity, creativity, fun, and vitality begin to slip away.

Internalized pain eventually becomes overwhelming and too much for the individual to handle alone. Since the individual cannot deal with pain externally, he or she develops an internal system to cope with it. For safety, protection, and survival, the person develops another voice or coping mechanism to help him or her deal with the pain: The *Protector* is born.

The Protector uses specific behaviors such as drinking, working, gambling, and overeating to cope with pain and stay away from uncomfortable feelings. Its behaviors help the person cope, survive, and even achieve greatness. The Protector is highly functional. For example, in a family affected by alcoholism, the children usually take on specific Protector roles to survive the pain of the disease. One child may become the comedian and provide humor to lighten up the tension. The humorous behavior will assist the child in dealing with his or her own pain. As an adult, however, this coping mechanism will likely begin to work against the individual if it becomes the primary way of dealing with woundedness.

There is a direct proportion between the amount of internalized pain and the power of the Protector. What this means is the intensity of the defense mechanism equals the severity of the trauma. When the wounded part and the protective part are dominant in a person's life, the True Self gets lost. It's as if the True Self is hidden behind two large walls. When people reach this level, they often say they have lost themselves. What many people don't understand is the Protector is not evil or bad. The Protector is a survival mechanism to help us cope with pain, yet these survival skills eventually turn against us and cause internal trauma. Emotional pain is like water in a swimming pool. The more emotional pain, the deeper below the surface the voice of the soul is placed. It becomes a whisper and barely heard. When the swimming pool is drained, the voice of the True Self can be heard.

The True Self is the magical child with all the passion, soul, and creativity. It intuitively knows how to handle life and it knows its purpose on earth. The True Self is present in people at birth but is suppressed by internalized emotional pain. When a family environment provides emotional safety, the True Self voice remains strong through childhood and adolescence.

Exercise

Now that we have discussed the formation of the voices, we will ask you a few questions to help you begin to identify your voices.

1. List three behaviors you do when you are feeling stressed.
2. List three incidents that were very painful for you in your life.
3. List three things you love to do or are passionate about.

Whichever question was the easiest for you to answer indicates which voice has the most power. The first question is reflective of your Protector, the second question is about your Wounded Child, and the third is about your True Self. If the third question was difficult for you to answer, it may indicate your True Self is lost.

Letters From the Voices

One of the exercises we encourage our clients to do on a daily basis is called Letters From the Voices. In this exercise, the client allows each voice to write a page in their journal about anything. Just let the voice speak. It is an excellent way to separate and contain thoughts and behaviors. Throughout the book, we have included letters from the voices from some of our clients. The following is an example of a man named John, whose Protector is The Scammer and Wounded Child is Teddy Bear.

The Protector: The Scammer (John)

I don't like life one bit. It's a place to either win or loose and there is no in between. I will win at all cost. If I have to lie, cheat, manipulate, or steal, I will do it to win. I hate feelings. They make life uncomfortable. You know, I like to get rid of feelings. Drinking is a great way to get away from feel-

18

ings. If I want a quick fix, I'll use cocaine. Up my nose and life is great. Ever since I stopped using alcohol and cocaine, I got hooked on those cigarettes, a smooth way to sedate.

I can't stand change. It sucks. If I change and get out of my routine, life becomes somewhat vulnerable and, you know, I need to avoid being vulnerable. What's the opposite of vulnerable? It's control. Yes, control! Control at all cost is what I like. Dominion and control. I love a relationship that is based on control much better than one based on love. Maintaining the upper hand is the battle that I engage in.

I really don't like to take chances. If I take a chance and don't succeed than I have to deal with the F word. Failure. I don't even like to say it. That's why I give up all my hopes and dreams, because I won't have to feel the possibility of failure. Every time John comes up with an idea, I criticize it, make fun of it, tell him it's foolish, and convince him to forget it. Complacency is the key to safe living. I am not concerned about quality of life; I desire survival and no pain.

The Wounded Child: Teddy Bear (John)

People think I am rough and tough because they see The Scammer most of the time, but underneath I am really soft as a Teddy Bear. I carry all of John's pain. The feeling I carry the most is fear. I am scared of everything. I use to be scared of my dad because he used to whip me and my brothers. Overall, he was a nice man, but he was distant—somewhere on another planet even though we lived in the same house. I tried all kinds of ways to get him close to me—make good grades, play sports, be good in school. It did not work. He used to deal with me when I got in trouble. In a weird way, his spankings and ragging at me was better than no attention at all. I love my daddy; I wish he would love me the way I think about him.

I don't like to be criticized. If people criticize me, it means they don't love me. Feeling unloved is like dying to me. I just want to be loved!

Woman are curious. I need them so badly, yet I can't stand the thought of being smothered. The most painful thing in the world is the thought of being abandoned by a woman. Who will take care of me? That is why I keep John in relationships he is not happy with because the abandonment is too much to handle. I don't let them get too close either. It is a delicate balance I am safe with, neither too close nor too far. If she withdraws, I get The Scammer to buy some flowers and promise I am going to change. If she gets too close, I get Scammer to pick a fight and push her away. It's like a game to keep her ten feet away. If she moves in, Scammer pushes, and if she pulls away, Scammer pulls. Scammer really does protect me from being hurt again.

True Self: John

I love you both, Teddy Bear and Scammer. When you two are calling the shots, I am very lonely. I am glad you two are talking to me. I finally understand why I act the way I do with other people. The only way for us to let go of fear is to trust in God. God is the morning sun that will keep us warm day and night. Even the jaws of death can't destroy us if we have God.

Teddy Bear, you are precious to me. I am sorry you feel so scared of being abandoned. I am a thirty-five-year-old man, and I will take care of you regardless of what other people do. Our girlfriend can leave, our friends can go away, our parents can reject us forever, and you will still have me and God to take care of you.

It is okay for us to receive constructive criticism today. If it is abusive, we will get support from our closest friends. The only criticism worth valuing is the criticism of people who love us. All the rest, we must let go. You are loved today if we succeed or if we fail; the warmth of our soul is there if we remain open to it.

Scammer, you have gotten me into all kinds of trouble and you have talked me into letting go of all my dreams. You don't have to protect Teddy Bear anymore. I am a thirty-five-year-old man, and I will take care of Teddy Bear. It is okay to take chances and risks because in the long run the successes and failures don't really matter anyway. The effort and desire are what is important.

I know cigarettes are the last big frontier of sedation. We are going to work on quitting. I know you will be very angry when we quit. I can handle the energy that will surface from internalized feelings. I will let you rant and rave about the things you hate by drawing and journaling, but I will not let you control my life. I want to have an intimate relationship and a successful job, and I will not let you sabotage these endeavors anymore. I love you.

CHAPTER 5

The Protector

Characteristics of the Protector

I See Red

Don't take away my drugs, they keep me at bay
Drinking helps me get through this lonely day
Don't take away my drugs, I need them to slow
Down the volcano inside, I'm going to blow.

I See Red, I See Red, what's come over me,
Rage at the world, uncontrollable scares me

Don't take away my job, it gives me life
I can buy many things for my kids and wife
Don't take away my job, I can't let go
If I slow down, I'm going to blow.

I See Red, I See Red, what's come over me,
Rage at the world, uncontrollable scares me

Don't take away my religion, human I'm not
Pray away my feelings, anger must stop
Don't take away my religion, God under my control
Get rid of emotion, what an unholy goal.

I See Red, I See Red, what's come over me,
Rage at the world, uncontrollable scares me

Don't take away my lover, can't live without sex
The chase keeps me going, I don't want to rest
Don't take away my lover, release the load
If I stop having sex, I will explode.

I See Red, I See Red, what's come over me,
Rage at the world, uncontrollable scares me

Don't take away my fantasy, it keeps me fooled
If I glance at reality, I'll become unglued
Don't take away my fantasy, I can't leave the fold
They taught me so well, keep under control.

I See Red, I See Red, what's come over me,
Rage at the world, uncontrollable scares me

The Protector is like a thief in the night who steals away the True Self. The Protector keeps us from painful feelings. Born in childhood and maturing in adolescence, it is a coping mechanism that uses many different behaviors, thoughts, and reactions to defend us from being hurt. It must be remembered initially the Protector is something good. Dean recalls a young man who told him a story about his father beating him regularly. One day he made the decision not to cry anymore after a beating, and he has not cried up to this day. Dean realized his Protector came to life on the day this young man quit crying. He developed the skills to dissociate from the physical pain of the beating and the emotional trauma of parental betrayal. Instead of the pain being externalized through the tears, the young boy internalized it, keeping it hidden in the cavity of his body. The lack of safety caused the boy to keep the pain behind a protective facade rather than expressing it.

The Protector is a voice that develops a belief system and language. Internalizing one's parents at their worst is part of the Protector. The healthy messages from the parents become part of the True Self while the unhealthy thoughts, reactions, and behaviors of a person's primary caretaker becomes part of their Protector. The primary caretakers may or may not be involved in the individual's life, yet the unhealthy messages live on in their Protectors.

The voice of the Protector crystallizes during adolescence. This voice either takes on the characteristics of the parent's Protectors or totally rejects them and takes on the opposite characteristics. When the family system is not healthy, the adolescent does not have the freedom to challenge the family belief systems; therefore, the adolescent is forced to repeat it or reject it totally. For example, a young boy who grew up in a rigid, military family will develop a Protector who either becomes a rigid, authoritarian parent or a liberal parent with no rules. A young girl who was forced to attend an oppressive Christian school she hated will insist her children go to this same type of school.

Here are a few other examples:

> "Being an artist is impractical," rings out in the head of a man who wants to try painting. It is the exact message his father told him thirty years previously.

> "You need a man to take care of you," a woman tells herself after her husband stayed out all night on a drinking binge.

> "Big boys aren't supposed to cry," a man tells his five-year-old son. The man can recall being told this as a young boy after his best friend moved to another city.

> "Women are not supposed to express their anger," rings out in a woman's mind after a shopper cut in front of her.

At different points in people's lives, the Protector begins to work against the soul. Because the Protector is trying to cope with the pain of the present and the past, the True Self gets lost behind the coping mechanism. As the pain increases, the Protector becomes more and more powerful. It needs to or the individual would not be able to function. Dysfunction is not the inability to function. It is functioning with large amounts of internalized pain or, in our language, with a very powerful Protector.

One of the ways Dean's Protector copes with uncomfortable feelings is isolation. Dean used to take long walks along the lake and think out his problems. This Protector behavior worked well for him, but when he became an adult, it began to work against him. Every time Dean got into a difficult situation, he would isolate, think, and withdraw. This appeared to be a healthy way to deal with pain, but Dean did not externalize it and have it validated. The emotional energy was pacified temporarily but contributed to the internal baggage. The baggage increased and Dean's Protector became more powerful. Every time he had a disagreement with HollyKem, his Protector wanted to isolate and never discuss the disagreement. Isolation and denial are not good for a relationship.

The Protector or Defender was created to help us deal with internalized pain. It will go to great lengths–even to the extent of physical, emotional, and spiritual suicide–to cut off anything that appears threatening. HollyKem recalls going to an emergency room that was filled with people. There was someone suffering from a drug overdose; another person had been in a car accident caused by a drunk driver. There was the gun shot wound that resulted from a drug deal. Down the hall was an anorexic young woman dying from malnutrition next to an obese man complaining of chest pains. The second floor of the hospital had an older woman with emphysema who was begging for a cigarette. An attractive business man in another room was taking a stress test because of his exhaustion. The third floor had a neonatal nursery with a crack baby and a man down the hall dying from full-blown AIDS. The fourth floor had a penniless gambler struggling to survive from a suicide attempt as well as a swollen alcoholic with a failing liver. Eating, drinking, gambling, sex, drugging, smoking, starving, and working are a few of the Protector behaviors that can cause physical, emotional, and spiritual suicide. When the Protector is in control, the self-destruction can be quick or it can be suicide by inches.

Mighty Protector

I know you hate the world and all its people,
You quiet down the crying voice inside my head.
Shut down my emotion, so that I won't be noticed.
Killing off my spirit keeps me far away from them.

I Am the Mighty Protector
Push away the people, so they won't hurt you.

You think money's evil, 'cause it can't buy love,
Beautiful mansions, marble floors cold as ice.
Pretty cars can't heal the longings of the soul,
So you destroy success, in the hopes of finding love.

I Am the Mighty Protector
Push away the people, so they won't hurt you.

You stay away from friends, 'cause they may see you.
Loneliness is better than the fear of being known.
Building walls of anger to protect the feeble castle,
A kingdom invaded by a silent enemy.

I Am the Mighty Protector
Push away the people, so they won't hurt you.

You can play the game of life without taking chances,
The safest way is the best way to keep me barely alive.
Did you know the road to Hell is fearful possession,
Afraid to love is the devil's best friend.

I Am the Mighty Protector
Push away the people, so they won't hurt you.

Codependency and Addiction

Can't Stop Thinking About It

Can't Stop Thinking About It
Can't Stop Thinking About It

Can't stop thinking 'bout the Snow
The snow they call the Rock
Got my mind all twisted up,
Can't stop thinking 'bout the Rock
Oh Lord, Lord, set me free
Oh Lord, set me Free

Can't Stop Thinking About It
Can't Stop Thinking About It

Stealing 10 from my Mom,
Stealing 20 from my friend.
Selling everything I got,
Just to crack up my head
Oh Lord, Lord, set me free
Oh Lord, set me Free

Can't Stop Thinking About It
Can't Stop Thinking About It

Lost my family to the snow,
Respect crushed by the Rock.
Lost my job and my dough,
My craving mind won't stop.
Oh Lord, Lord, set me free
Oh Lord, set me Free

Can't Stop Thinking About It
Can't Stop Thinking About It

My conscience is now dead,
Flame of my soul almost out.
I'll gun down my brother dead,
Just to worship the Rock.
Oh Lord, Lord, set me free
Oh Lord, set me Free

Can't Stop Thinking About It
Can't Stop Thinking About It

Some Protectors become addicted; however, this was not the original intention. In our practice we work with many people who call themselves codependents and addicts. Our definition of codependency is protective behaviors that keep us out of our pain, out of our feelings, and out of our body. All addicts are codependent but not all codependents become addicts.

As a seventeen-year-old girl, HollyKem's Protector progressed to the level of addiction. HollyKem believed she could drink, drug, and starve herself without consequence. She was not in touch with her soul or her body; she had no idea who she was. She was in touch only with her Protector voice, and she thought that was all there was to her. She believed she was bad and alone.

How did HollyKem get to this point? She had lost her trust in the adults in her family and her community. She needed someone or something to help her cope. She felt she could not trust anyone outside of herself, so she turned inward to someone who would protect her and give her relief. Consequently, HollyKem learned to depend on her Defender.

She bought her Protector's belief system that said, "No pain, at any cost, even if it means self-destruction. I don't need people. Life sucks. Die young." She has paid a huge price for buying into this belief system.

To help simplify and identify our Protectors, we encourage our clients to name their Protector. HollyKem calls hers C.M., which stands for Control Monster. When this part of HollyKem is in control, C.M., who hates everything, uses anger to manipulate.

Addiction is not something a person chooses, but it is something from which someone *suffers*. We believe all addictions are ways to help a person cope with his or her pain. The Protector is the addict. The Protector is the belief system that says, "If you use . . . (drugs, food, work, alcohol, gambling, sex, religion, nicotine, television, bulimia, starvation, sports, sugar), there will be no pain." This is the lie that keeps many people in bondage. It temporarily works but eventually catches up to you. The most common way an individual quits one addiction is by switching to another. The bondage continues; it just has a different face.

What is the price one pays when the Protector behavior is taken away? *Rage!* Rage at me, rage at you, rage at them, rage at the world. If someone took away your best friend or your most precious ally, you would become angry. When you take away your Protector's behavior, you take away its purpose, and he or she will not be happy about this. After the rage, the internalized feelings begin to surface. It's emotionally overwhelming when the self-destructive behavior is contained. It is very frightening to work with the internalized feelings. For too long the Protector has dealt with the pain, and the pain has trusted the Protector. It is time to learn a new way to nurture the pain.

There is a common phenomena we call the functioning addict/alcoholic. This describes the person who is chemically addicted to alcohol or drugs, yet functions at a high level in the eyes of society. This person could be well liked in the community and have a family, a good job, and financial success. In reality, however, this person experiences emotional and spiritual agony. This person is lonely! The Protector is in *control*. Many functioning alcoholics go unnoticed, except to the people closest to them.

* * * * *

America, America land of the Free
Free to choose your Own Slavery

* * * * *

The Protector is the compulsive voice. It demands that the individual be perfect, clean, thin, busy, and right. Obsession is the rule. This type of defender keeps the person in the head and out of the feelings. The obsessive thoughts keep the person stuck in the grief process, sandwiched between anger and pain. (Refer back to the grief process discussion in Chapter 4.) This individual is *not* in the *body*, and *nobody* is allowed too close. When the obsession gets too strong, it is time to react.

Many people suffer tremendously when the Protector screams inside the mind. "If" stands for I-Fault. I-Fault means that during the bargaining of the grief process, the individual blames themselves or others for the loss. Some examples are listed as follows:

- If I had been a better lover , he would not have had the affair.

- If I would have quit nagging him, he would not have had the heart attack.

- If I was a better son, my dad would like me.
- If I worked harder, I would be happy.
- If I was thinner, I would be married.
- If I was less emotional, I would have more friends.

These thought processes talk, scream, and whisper and keep us from sleeping at night, working during the day, and being able to love our children at times. When obsession is rampant in the mind, it is an internal war waged at an elusive enemy. Many suffer when the Protector acts, yet it is just as painful when the Protector does not stop talking inside one's head. The payoff is staying out of the feelings, but the price is a thundering storm inside the head. Individuals who stop acting out addictively often shift to compulsive thinking.

Family Roles

In a family system affected by an addictive cycle, the members of the family usually take on clearly defined roles. An addictive cycle means the family has addiction in the immediate or extended family. The family members take on roles that form the foundation of the Protector. Very seldom do individuals stay in one role, yet one is often dominant. Even if the family has no history of addiction, children may take these roles if the family has experienced some trauma such as death, divorce, or sexual abuse. When the family is emotionally shut down for any reason, the children will take on these roles. The roles are the Clown, the Overachiever, the Problem Child, the Absent Child, the Caretaker, the Peacemaker, and the Surrogate Spouse.

The Clown is the child who uses humor to stop the tension or distract from the pain in the family. At school, this child is known as the class clown. Fear is the motivating feeling behind the behavior. This person is usually emotionally immature and has a difficult time being serious as an adult.

The Overachiever is the child who excels in whatever he or she becomes involved, such as grades, sports, and leadership. Inadequacy is the motivator behind the overachievement. This person brings honor and prestige to the family. He or she is usually financially successful as an adult, and sometimes is a compulsive worker.

The Problem Child breaks rules and tries to show the community there is something wrong in the family system. Most people believe anger is the motivating feeling, but it is actually hurt. This child becomes the focus of the family while the other important problems are ignored. As an adult, this person will self-destruct if he or she maintains this role.

The Absent Child is the passive, quiet individual who rarely makes any waves. This child understands the problems in the family, yet chooses to withdraw by using fantasy to escape reality. This person will avoid conflict and shy away from social situations. Loneliness is the motivator. As an adult, this individual likes to be alone. Of all the roles, this child is most likely to commit suicide.

The Caretaker is the child who takes on many responsibilities in the family. This is "Little Mom" or "Little Dad." This child takes on parental eyes by attempting to discipline other siblings, caretaking a parent or performing domestic duties at a very early age. This child is motivated by worthlessness and as an adult is attracted to the helping professions and needy people.

The Peacemaker is the child who tries to keep the peace. This child is sensitive and docile and a good mediator. Terror of potential conflict and abuse is the motivator. This person is attracted to social activist organizations as an adult.

The Surrogate Spouse is the child who bonds with a parent in an adult, emotional way. The generational boundaries between this child and the parent are unclear. The parent gets his or her spousal needs met through the child instead of another adult. As an adult, this person usually repeats this cycle. The motivator is the fear of being smothered.

Sometimes an individual takes on more than one role or will switch roles in the family. For example, a child may have been an Absent Child until the teenage years when he or she became the Problem Child. Characteristics of the roles are not all bad. The Clown develops a wonderful sense of humor. The roles are the problem because they are a reaction to the emotional pain in the family. Being stuck in a role means being possessed by the Protector.

Emotional Bullets

The Protector keeps one out of pain. We use the term *triggered* to describe when an incident brings unresolved pain from the past to the surface. When you are triggered, it feels like you have been shot by an emotional bullet. The Protector will do anything to defend the person from being triggered, and after the emotional bullet, the Protector will try to stop the internal agony. How does the Protector do this? Raging, fighting, hitting, using drugs, drinking, running, eating, isolating, hiding, and fixing to name a few. It's a *possession*. When the Protector takes over, the mind and body are at the mercy of the Protector's beliefs.

Lisa was just hit by an emotional bullet. Her boyfriend told her he wants to date other women, but they could still be friends. Lisa's Protector, Miss Piggy, likes to use compulsive eating to deal with her pain. In this situation, Miss Piggy comes to the rescue. She goes home and eats and eats and eats. As much as Lisa tries to stop, Miss Piggy wins the battle and continues to eat. This is full-blown *possession*. Now if Miss Piggy could not find food, she would substitute another behavior to control the pain. This is a subconscious process difficult to identify. Lisa is the one who suffers when Miss Piggy gets control. The tragedy is Lisa believes Miss Piggy is her True Self. Self-hatred is the result.

Coupleship is the one institution that brings out the Protector more than any other. When a person is triggered by his or her significant other, the intensity of the emotion is often about unresolved pain from the past more than the present situation. People say and do things in coupled relationships they never imagined was possible. They are *out of control,* one of the primary characteristics of the Protector.

John and Mary have been married for four years. John gets very angry when Mary comes home a few minutes late from work. He screams and then pouts the rest of the night. Mary does not understand why John's intensity of anger is so strong because she is just a few minutes late. This cycle is repeated over and over, and it becomes a major problem in their marriage. John's Protector uses screaming and pouting to control his wife from being late. John believes the intensity of his anger is only about Mary being late.

When John and Mary came into counseling, Dean found out John grew up with an alcoholic father. Many nights, John's father would get home late from work because he stopped at a bar. When his father arrived home late, John's parent had a major fight. The trigger is a spouse coming home late from work. John's Protector believes if he can keep his wife from coming home late, he will not have to feel the unresolved pain from the past.

Rage

When the Wounded Child is triggered, the Protector responds with rage. Rage is a storehouse of emotional energy that yearns for expression. If the emotional energy is not embraced in a healthy manner, it is acted out in a destructive behavior. The destruction may be directed toward another person or it may be directed toward oneself. Hitting, fighting, and screaming are examples of raging outward; starving, addiction, and depression are examples of raging inward. Protector behavior acts out the storehouse of energy and causes devastation.

Don't Want to Live

Static from movement, safe as can be
Cut off from the World, especially you and me.
Can't afford to be hurt, the price is too high
Wish I didn't live on earth, want to live in the sky.

Don't want to live, too scared to die,
Livin's a burden, numb out inside.

Burden to my family, so I live independently
Closing the channels that lead to prosperity.
Guarding the Soul, its cold inside,
Can't depend on no one except my false pride.

Don't want to live, too scared to die,
Livin's a burden, numb out inside.

God is in my head, distant from my heart,
Nice idea to treasure, especially the day I depart.
The castle of my Soul has rejected its maker,
Defended at all cost, a hellish creation.

Don't want to live, too scared to die,
Livin's a burden, numb out inside.

Livin' in a fantasy, the truth's too much to bear,
Passing up love, because of my fear.
Gettin' old and got nowhere, except this lonely road,
Pay the Pauper one more time, what's lost is my Soul.

Don't want to live, too scared to die,
Livin's a burden, numb out inside.

Exercise

The following exercise will help you identify and name your Protector. Answer the following questions as best you can. Base your answers on your own understanding of the questions. There is no right or wrong answer.

1. What are compulsive behaviors you have now or have had in the past? If you have any addictions, write these down.

2. When you were a child, what did you do to cope with painful feelings?

3. As an adult, what behaviors do you do to avoid painful feelings?

4. In your relationships, what do you do to keep people at a distance?

5. Name as many incidents as you remember, as an adolescent or adult, when you broke your value system or broke the law, or when you sinned.

6. Name an incident or incidents when you people-pleased and did something you really did not want to do.

7. Name an experience when you made someone else more important than yourself and hurt yourself by doing so.

8. Who did you protect the most in the family—mother, father, sibling, friends, or a pet?

9. As an adolescent, what was your greatest accomplishment? What was your worst failure?

10. As an adolescent, what did you do to feel good about yourself?

11. As an adolescent, how did you deal with painful feelings?

12. As an adolescent, what did you do with your peers to get attention?

13. At what age did you first have sexual intercourse?

14. What was your physical and emotional image of yourself as an adolescent?

15. In your family of origin, what role or roles in the family did you have—the Clown, the Overachiever, the Problem Child, the Absent Child, the Caretaker, the Peacemaker, and/or the Surrogate Spouse?

Go back and read over your answers. You have just identified your Protector. Let your mind and soul be open to a name. You can change your name anytime, so don't wait for the perfect name. Here are some of the names our clients have given to their Protectors: Terminator, Nirvana, Fury, Demus, Blurr, FeFe, Scammer, Brain Dead, Lona, Slickster, Vanilla, Fudge, Jack Daniels, Coconut, Janis Joplin, Gangus Slickameyer, Pitt Bull, St. Francis, Pac Man, J.R., and Kawasaki. Fill out the picture on the next page with your Protector's name.

One of the most difficult things for people to understand is the Protector was built for survival and as a reaction to help deal with one's woundedness. It is very important for you to learn and understand your Protector completely. From its

Name of your protector

origin to the present time, you must intellectually understand its formation so you can embrace it lovingly. Having a Protector has produced many losses, but it also has produced many gains. In an effort to help you understand your Protector more completely, do the following exercise.

Exercise

Look back at the answers you gave in the preceding exercise. Based on what you have just learned about your Protector, write down in your notebook the losses and gains associated with your Protector. The purpose of the exercise is to realize that your Protector has provided you with some gains, but also has caused great suffering for the soul. In one column, list the losses you have experienced when your Protector has been in control. In the other column, list the gains you have experienced when your Protector has been in control. We have included an example of a person who has done this.

Tom is a recovering alcoholic who has liver problems because of his excessive use of alcohol. Divorced with two children, Tom is a very successful businessman who is presently struggling with compulsive working. Tom named his Protector Draino.

Losses	Gains
My wife	Good business
My marriage	Money
A family	Charmer
My children on a daily basis	Ambitious
My health	Ability to think quickly
Self-respect	Compassion
Money	Twelve Steps
Friends	Work ethic
Trust	Organization skills
Hope	Depth
Intimacy	Charisma
My soul	Ability to adjust
Values	
Confidence	
Sex	
God	
Relaxation	
Integrity	
Brain cells	
Time	
Love	

Letters From the Voices

The Protector: Starvy (Karen)

I hate everybody and everything. I hate little Karen's parents because they abandoned her, and I hate the friends who emotionally and verbally abused her. I trust no one. When little Karen trusted people in the past, they lied to her and disappointed her. When her feelings were so overwhelming she thought they would kill her, I came to her rescue. When she was so mad but did not have a safe place to express her anger, I taught her to throw it up. Throwing up helped her numb out and temporarily relieve her pain. When she felt afraid or sad, I taught her to starve herself. A starving person can't feel anything–not fear, sadness, joy, or happiness. My ultimate goal is to kill Karen so little Karen won't have to face the world and all of its scary responsibilities. I am the voice inside Karen's head that says things like, "Don't eat." "Be afraid of food." "You don't deserve to eat." I am happy when she skips meals or loses weight because I know we are one step closer to death.

The Wounded Child: Little Karen (Karen)

I am a scared little girl. As far back as I can remember I was always scared of everybody and everything. I was afraid Dad would come home drunk again and start screaming and throwing things and threatening to leave. I was afraid Mom would get depressed and take another overdose, and I would be an orphan. Who would take care of me? Who would love me, feed me, and tuck me in at night? I cry all the time. I always feel sad, lonely, and helpless. All I want to do is crawl in bed with my stuffed animals and go to sleep so I won't have to feel anything or face all the scary people and places in the world. I wish they would go away and leave me alone. Sometimes I want to die, but most of the time I just want somebody to hug me and tell me they love me and that everything is going to be okay.

The True Self: Karen (Thirty-Two-Year-Old Woman)

I hear you Little Karen. I hear your fear and sadness. You had a lot to be fearful and sad about when you were a little girl. There was no safe place to go to be yourself and no one to talk to about your pain, but I am here for you today. I am listening, and I'll allow you to feel your feelings. I'll take care of you. I'll love you and nurture you and put my arms around you and tell you everything is going to be okay. I will no longer be paralyzed by your fear. I will not avoid taking risks and making changes just because you are afraid. Part of experiencing life and happiness means taking risks and making changes to improve the quality of my life. Today I will face my fears and take positive action, knowing I am being guided by a loving, caring God. We are not alone anymore.

I hear you, Starvy. I hear your anger and rage. You have every right to be angry at the people who abandoned and abused Little Karen. I'm grateful you were able to protect her when she was little because I did not know how, but those old coping behaviors aren't working anymore. They are robbing me of a happy, healthy life and slowly, painfully driving me to an early grave. Today, I refuse to give in to self-destruction. Instead of starving or throwing up, I am going to therapy and twelve-step meetings. I am learning to give my body the nutrition it deserves. In the process, I am learning how to love myself and enjoy life one day at a time.

CHAPTER 6

The Wounded Child

Let It Rain

Characteristics of the Wounded Child

Let It Rain

There was a little boy back in school
Scared to tell the teacher about her broken rules.
Lil' Johnny bursting with pain,
Don't want to go to school, sure hope it rains.

Let it rain, let it rain
Tears on the ground
Let it rain, let it rain
Wash away the shame

Little boy, confused in his room

45

Inside the screaming won't quiet down
Holds down the volume, behind a facade
A storm is brewing, inside his mind

> Let it rain, let it rain
> Tears on the ground
> Let it rain, let it rain
> Wash away the shame

Little boy, scared to say
They won't believe me anyway
Mama loves me, Daddy too
Yet, I don't know what to do

> Let it rain, let it rain
> Tears on the ground
> Let it rain, let it rain
> Wash away the shame

Little boy can't become a man
Haunted by the works of an evil man
Planted grief deep in his soul
Don't know how to let it go

> Let it rain, let it rain
> Tears on the ground
> Let it rain, let it rain
> Wash away the pain

Ann is a married twenty-five-year-old woman who does not understand why she does not want to have sex with her husband. When Ann was a little girl, she was molested by her uncle on many occasions. When this trauma occurred, it was not safe for her to talk about it with her family. *Ann lost her voice.* Her feelings of betrayal, shame, hurt, confusion, and fear were stored inward. Now, the part we call the Wounded Child is interfering with Ann's adult sex life.

The Wounded Child is the part of us that carries our pain. If it was not safe to externalize the pain when the incident occurred, we hold it in the Wounded Child. In the case of Ann, she has stored her pain about being molested, and this pain is triggered when she thinks about being sexual with her husband.

Two of the most important characteristics of the Wounded Child is that it has *no sense of time* and *thinks symbolically*. No sense of time means there is no distinction between past, present, and future. An emotional event that occurred twenty years ago feels like it happened yesterday. Any unresolved pain about a particular issue can be triggered and brought to the surface. Ann is in a safe environment with her husband, so her Wounded Child is trying to have a voice by her reaction in a sexual situation.

Thinking symbolically means the Wounded Child thinks in symbols. For Ann, the symbol is a significant, male family member who wants to be sexual with her. Ann's Wounded Child does not know the difference between her uncle and her husband. Until Ann realizes what is going on internally, she will continue to have sexual problems with her husband.

Triggered and Possessed

Just as the Protector can possess the mind and body, so can the Wounded Child. When the Wounded Child takes over, one regresses to a younger age and *feels like a child*. The regression can bring one back emotionally to infancy through later childhood. Some common triggers that create this possession are angry people, authority, abandonment, fear, violence, and embarrassment. Very often, people cannot speak when the Wounded Child takes over. This is when people know that they lost themselves. And they have. However, their solution is to get rid of the trigger instead of embracing the internal issue. *It's an inside job!*

When the Wounded Child is triggered, we tend to react to situations with more intensity than what is normal. Like most men, Dean's Wounded Child (Bopper) has a fear of being smothered by a woman. One day, HollyKem said to Dean with excitement, "I took the whole weekend off, and we can be together for two days." On the surface, Dean tried to be happy, but Bopper was terrified. The intensity of the fear did not equal the outside situation. Dean was possessed by his Wounded Child. The intensity of his emotion was more about his fear of being smothered than it was about spending a weekend with HollyKem. It is very important for Dean to realize this so he doesn't sabotage the weekend. It also is a sign that Dean needed to explore his history and allow Bopper to talk about why he is terrified.

Remember our discussion about emotional bullets in the previous chapter? Emotional bullets are when our Wounded Child is triggered. It does not take much to trigger our woundedness. A crooked glance, a shaming statement, a negative comment, or just being ignored are a few examples that could push our buttons. After the button is pushed, we must search for the symbol and allow the Wounded Child to talk.

The Wounded Child and the Protector are intimately related. They are buddies. The Protector is like an older brother, a bully, a Momma or Papa Bear that needs to guard the little one. If the little one is triggered, you can be sure of a reaction by the Protector.

What are some indications of being possessed by the Wounded Child?

- All-or-nothing thinking
- Controlling phobias

- Feelings one is very young or regressed
- Overwhelming emotions
- No voice
- Blind obedience
- Using "always, never, forever" when talking
- Unexplained pain or fear
- Believing everything is about *me*

The Wounded Child and the Magical Child

It is important to remember the Wounded Child and the Magical Child are different. The Wounded Child holds the hurts that were internalized and did not have a voice. The Magical Child is the part that carries the happy, joyful, good memories of the past. One does not discount the other. However, if the Wounded Child is not embraced, the Magical Child will be lost. On the other hand, when the Wounded Child is given a voice, the Magical Child will spontaneously surface while an individual experiences a new-found freedom.

Sometimes people *only* remember the good from the past; others are stuck in the anger and *only* see the wounds of the past. In both of these cases, the Protector is in control. For those who see only the good, the Protector is keeping that person from being in touch with his or her woundedness. In the second case, the Protector keeps a person stuck in his or her anger so it keeps others at a distance.

Emotion
Life Is a Game
The Shameful blackness in the pit of my stomach
It began to grow many years ago
Violated, exposed to a preying mantis

Want to shed my skin, can't let it go.

Life is the game that creates emotion
My body is the temple where energy flows
Death is the price for stored up feeling,
Free your body and soul, let the energy go.

The fearful constriction tightening my chest
In a world of uncertainty, it began to grow
Childlike terror in the body of a man.
Want to shed my skin, can't let it go.

Life is the game that creates emotion
My body is the temple where energy flows
Death is the price for stored up feeling,
Free your body and soul, let the energy go.

The angry explosion, caught in my throat
Pent up for years behind a saintly glow.
My mind is fighting this volcanic energy.
Want to shed my skin, can't let it go.

Life is the game that creates emotion
My body is the temple where energy flows
Death is the price for stored up feeling,
Free your body and soul, let the energy go.

The saddening rivers pounding in my head
Years of losses made it grow
Will the dam break and flow forever
Want to shed my skin, can't let it go.

Life is the game that creates emotion
My body is the temple where energy flows
Death is the price for stored up feeling,
Free your body and soul, let the energy go.

In working with the Wounded Child, we help our clients release painful emotions. *E-motion,* which is energy in motion, must be released safely and expressed in a healthy manner or it will *kill.* Painful emotion is like a train running throughout the body. The train is activated by some kind of trigger and starts running. The train runs through the arms, the legs, the stomach and heart, the head and back–and it keeps on running. Sometimes it gets stuck. In the stomach, it causes ulcers. In the heart, it causes a heart attack. In the head, it causes migraines. In the back, it causes stiff shoulders.

Instead of the train taking us for a ride, we must command and own it. It belongs to us. We must work with it and let it have some type of healthy expression. The only way to release the train is to give it a voice in a safe environment. Verbal, written, and artistic expression are different ways to give it a voice. *Your wounded child must have a voice!*

When years of painful emotions are stored in the body, the results are devastating. Can you imagine trying to contain a raging tornado inside a large tent? It will rumble, move, and eat away at the sides of the tent. Many of us contain this raging tornado for many years. In fact, a tremendous amount of energy is taken to hold the storm back. Depression is the result! Eventually the tent will bust open. A rage attack! We have all experienced this raging tornado. Woundedness happens when we interact with people who are carrying raging tornadoes inside. They will abuse by attacking or withdrawing, causing a tornado inside of us. The cycle perpetuates. With the Voices Within, the Wounded Child is the tornado and the Protector acts it out.

In our practice clients believe they are going to die when they touch this tornado. The emotional intensity is overwhelming and scary. The reality is that the *emotion will not kill*–unless it is not embraced. This is when many clients leave therapy because it is so scary. What they don't realize, however, is they are on the verge of freedom.

Memory Loss

Many of our clients say they can't remember their childhoods. Some say they don't remember certain periods such as the time between ages five and ten. There is a reason we forget: *pain.* It is the Wounded Child that holds these memories along with painful emotions. Our Protector, who does not want us to feel pain, helps us conveniently forget. When the Protector is in control, the Wounded Child is not allowed to have a voice. The Protector does the same thing that was done in childhood–certain experiences were not talked about and certain feelings were not felt.

Traumatic Bonding

Can't Sleep at Night

Fallen down in the prime of life.
Married man leaves his wife.
Children, lost and confused
Who will buy the family food? Says the

Little boy, who can't sleep at night.
Cause he scared he's goin' to die.
Daddy come kiss me goodnight.
Come and kiss me one more time.
I don't want to say goodbye.
I don't want to say goodbye.

On the feast of St. Joseph Day.
Under Earth Daddy's put away.
See the priest wave to God.
Oh, I wonder will I survive, says the

Little boy, who can't sleep at night.
Cause he scared he's goin' to die.
Daddy come kiss me goodnight.
Come and kiss me one more time.
I don't want to say goodbye.
I don't want to say goodbye

Family and friends come and go.
Some I've never seen before.
All them wearing crying smiles.
Want to cry but I don't know how, says the

Little boy, who can't sleep at night.
Cause he scared he's goin' to die.
Daddy come kiss me goodnight.
Come and kiss me one more time.
I don't want to say goodbye.
I don't want to say goodbye

There is a phenomenon called traumatic bonding. What this means is when a person experiences a trauma, there is an emotional bonding to this experience. When a person experiences a traumatic event, the soul is torn. The healthy way of healing from the trauma is to talk about the details of the experience repeatedly. These emotions need to be validated in a safe context. The feelings will follow. The tear in the soul begins to be sewn up. When this doesn't happen, the Wounded Child holds the feelings and the soul remains torn. Traumatic bonding occurs when the trauma is recreated in your life.

HollyKem comes from a divorced family. The divorce itself was very traumatic for her. By the time she was six years old, HollyKem made a promise she would never have children and never get a divorce. Ethie, her Wounded Child, believes marriage is *abusive and scary.* By the time HollyKem was nineteen, she was married. The marriage was very *abusive and scary.* By the age of twenty-four, HollyKem was separated and awaiting divorce. She was bonded to the trauma of her parent's marriage and divorce, and C.M. (her Protector) recreated it in her life. The Protector will carry out the belief of the Wounded Child if the Wounded Child is not given a voice. HollyKem originally suffered from the actions of her parents–the external trauma, then suffered from her own actions–the recreated internal trauma. This cycle ended when Ethie was able to really tell her story. There is a direct relationship between Ethie (the Wounded Child) and C.M. (the Protector). HollyKem began to take the power away from her Protector when she let Ethie have a voice. Thankfully, the bondage about marriage was released.

Traumatic bonding also occurs when an experience is repeated over and over. Charles is a thirty-nine-year-old man who has been married three times. All three wives had affairs during the marriage. Each marriage ended by his wife leaving the relationship and divorcing him. Charles does not understand why this keeps happening because he loved his wives. He was adopted by a very loving family at birth and believed the adoption had no affect on him. His Wounded Child, who was trying to be heard, was carrying pain because he felt betrayed and abandoned by his biological mother (a significant woman in his life). As an adult, Charles was betrayed and abandoned by his wives (also significant women). This trauma is repeated over and over by the affairs and the divorces. Charles's Protector (The Great Prince) refuses to see how his neediness and possessiveness drive the woman in his life away.

The original trauma is external–Charles was given away by his mother. The Wounded Child's belief is "I am no good," so his Protector repeatedly picked someone emotionally and physically unavailable. This repetition is caused by the internal belief. Until Charles deals with the pain of being abandoned by his biological mother, he will continue to recreate this trauma, and the bondage continues.

Exercise

The following exercise will help you identify and name your Wounded Child. Answer the following questions as best you can. Base your answers on your own understanding of the questions. There is no right or wrong answer.

1. As a child, what painful feelings do you identify with most: fear, hurt, loneliness, sadness, depression, or anger?

2. What are the most painful experiences you had with your father?

3. What are the most painful experiences you had with your mother?

4. Name an event in grammar school that was particularly painful for you.

5. Where did you live when you were a child?

6. Name an event in high school that was particularly painful for you.

7. Did you have a pet? What was his or her name?

8. Describe an event or events when you felt very embarrassed.

9. Describe an event or events when you felt afraid.

10. If you were violated as a child or teenager, describe the incident.

11. Name an event during adulthood that was particularly painful for you.

12. What is the biggest loss you experienced as a child, as a teenager, and as an adult?

Go back and read over your answers. You have just identified your Wounded Child. Let your mind and soul be open to a name. You can change your name anytime, so don't wait for the perfect name. Here are some of the names our clients have given to their Wounded Child: Annie, Caroline, Spongy, Little Man, Ashley, T-boy, Treasure, Allison, Sadie, Pumpkin, Rose, Mickey, Dopey, and Tears. Fill out the following picture with your Wounded Child's name.

Name of your Wounded Child

CHAPTER 7

The True Self

At age nineteen, HollyKem was a drug dealer addicted to cocaine and physically in bad shape. Her Protector was in control and she appeared soulless to the rest of the world. *She appeared soulless to herself.* Although her Wounded Child was sedated by drugs, HollyKem was traumatized daily because of her lifestyle. The price she paid for her Protector being in control was and still is very high. She continues to suffer physically, even though it has been fifteen years without a drink or any drugs. It took HollyKem many years to understand her soul *is* her True Self. She learned to shut it out and discount it–to *not* trust her True Self. It spoke, but C.M., her Protector, spoke louder. She hated herself because she believed she was C.M. Her True Self was totally lost and she didn't know who she was.

Who Am I?

We must all answer the question, "Who am I?" We must discover who we really are, what we really want, what excites us, and what gives us life. This is the only way we can obtain freedom. Finding one's soul is a deep, intense, painful, and passionate journey. The hard part is the painful part. The True Self emerges spontaneously when we begin separating the Protector and the Wounded Child.

What Is the True Self?

The True Self is the *soul*, the *adult*, the *magic*, the *faithful*, the *limit setter*, and the *creator*. The True Self is the *parent* for the self and has the solutions. It is the *dreamer*, the *risk taker*, and the *peaceful one*. It looks into other people's eyes and is a *good listener*. It has a voice and gives us our purpose on earth.

When we are guarded and live in fear, we can never have a real sense of belonging. What we have is *loneliness*. Fear rules and creates doubt. The doubter inside each of us is either the Wounded Child or the Protector. When the doubter is in control, the soul cannot be heard. The voices of the Wounded Child and Protector need to be set aside so the True Self can speak. Once we separate our Wounded Child and Protector, we can hear the voice of our soul.

The True Self holds the solutions to life's problems and complexities. It has the natural ability to be in touch with God so one has the courage to accomplish what one is inspired to do. The True Self is level, alive, awake, and loving. It has vision and is not afraid to share it. It allows God's people to be! It does not need to fix them but to love them. The soul knows good from evil, love from hate, peace from obsession, moderation from addiction, and boundaries from control. The True Self is *kind, honest, and trusting*—to ourselves and others but first and foremost to God. The soul knows from whence it came.

I Have A Dream

I have a dream to live peacefully
Inside my skin, relief from the enemy
I have a dream, that cries out in the night
The secret passion, that make's life worthwhile

I have a dream, to look into the mirror
To be in love, with the person before me
I have a dream, to know that I am good
The eyes in the mirror, are lights of a precious soul

I have a dream, to die at peace with my God
Let go of my fear, the childish terror inside
I have a dream, to sing with life & love
To heal my neighbor and to be a channel for God's love

Do you have a dream, that stirs up your passion
The quiet little voice, that cries out in the night
Do you have a dream, don't let it go untold
Do you have a dream, God's message to your soul!

Origin of the True Self

The True Self is present when we are created. The Magical Child is the True Self at an early age. The True Self is the divine spark that pushes us to heal, grow, love, and create. A child who is in a safe environment spontaneously does these things. The greatest people in history maintained or redeveloped the ability to do these things: Great artists create, great saints love, great intellects grow, and great leaders heal. The True Self is lost because it is overpowered by the dynamic duo: the Protector and the Wounded Child. Pain is the powerful motivator of the duo, which can cause someone to appear soulless. The True Self needs to be nurtured and given a voice. If we don't have permission *to be*, our True Self voice is lost. It is there, but we must listen for it!

We are created by God, and the True Self holds the container of truth God intended us to be. By listening to our True Self voice, we can understand our uniqueness, our giftedness, our vision, our passion, and our destiny. Peace of mind and happiness come from listening and obeying our soul voice.

The True Self is the healthy part. It is the part that acts in an adult, healthy manner. It can communicate openly and honestly; it acts appropriately. The True Self is creative, spontaneous, and full of life. When you see someone in his or her True Self, this person radiates from within. People in their True Self seem to be grounded on earth, yet their vision expands to the clouds. The True Self is spiritual and connected with God in a very personal and real way. People in their True Self have a deep love for themselves; consequently, they can selflessly love others. They have taken the beliefs of family, society, and religion and brought them before the judgment of their conscience. They integrate the beliefs that make spiritual sense to their soul and live by them. *They are not ruled by fear!*

Soulful living is like having an internal family. The True Self is the parent, the Protector is the rebellious adolescent, while the Wounded Child is the needy little kid. Each of these family members within have their own belief system. The True Self is the part that needs to listen and understand the other two voices. For example, Ethie believes marriage is scary and abusive, C.M. believes marriage sucks and is a trap, and HollyKem's True Self believes it is a wonderful partnership to share life, dreams, pain, and hopes. By understanding the different belief systems, HollyKem was able to make a decision based on her True Self.

What is your True Self like? The following exercise will help you get in touch with your True Self. Let your mind be open, free, and creative without limits. Beware of your Protector telling you these things are impossible and silly.

Exercise

1. What are you most passionate about? What excites you? What brings you to life?

2. What does your ideal life look like?

> Job?
> Family?
> Home?
> Hobbies/activities?
> Friends?
> Lifestyle?

3. What are your dreams?

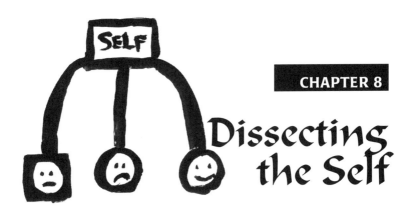

CHAPTER 8

Dissecting the Self

I BELIEVE

Separating the Voices

The purpose of identifying and separating the voices is to find *internal freedom*. How does one find the map to freedom? The first step is to identify destructive and self-defeating behaviors. This is our Protector. The second step is to find and embrace our woundedness, or our internalized pain. This is our Wounded Child. The third is to let the True Self have a voice and follow it.

Belief Systems

Each voice has an independent belief system. Once in a while, all three voices have the same beliefs about a particular subject. More often the beliefs differ, and this causes self-doubt, confusion, and inner turmoil. The reason our beliefs are so important is because all of our actions—conscious and unconscious—are grounded in a belief. Beneath all of our actions is some type of belief; we don't just spontaneously react. For example, when people scream or speak loudly, they do so because they believe nobody is listening. Some people don't talk at all because they believe their opinions are unimportant. Until we discover the belief that motivates our behavior, we will have a difficult time changing our behavior. The dissection process is to learn the convictions of each voice.

Each of the voices has its own belief and feelings about a particular subject. In the beginning of the dissecting process, we pick a variety of subjects and each voice gets to talk about its belief concerning the subject. We will use a thirty-four-year-old woman named Samantha to illustrate the dissecting process. Her Wounded Child is Sugar and her Protector is Dancing Magnolia. We encourage you to do the same exercise in a notebook, listing important subjects in your life.

Dissecting the Self

I Believe

Subject	Protector (Dancing Magnolia)	Wounded Child (Sugar)	True Self (Samantha, 34-yr.-old woman)
Marriage	Doesn't work	Is painful	I don't know
Life	Reality sucks, so party	It hurts me	Is more than what I'm doing
Money	Is power	Causes fights	Is necessary
Sex	A way to control	Terrifying	A way to express love
Home	Must be avoided	Is a battleground	A place for my family
Men	Must be kept away	Will hurt me	Are good friends
Women	Loves them	Loves them	Loves them

This is very important to understand. The belief systems are set up differently because of the unique history of the person. When Samantha experiences a *trauma*, she is *wounded*. She builds a *belief* because of the trauma, and she reacts out of this protection, which in the future causes *retraumatization*.

Trauma ▶ Wounded ▶ Belief ▶Retraumatization

Samantha was sexually abused by her stepfather between the ages five and eight (the trauma). She internalized feelings of shame, hatred, betrayal, fear, and hurt (the woundedness), Sugar (her Wounded Child) believes *all men will violate and hurt her* (the belief), and she becomes a stripper. It does not fit, but her Protector must find an environment where men *will violate and hurt her.* She needs to carry out the belief and the strip bar is the perfect place (retraumatization). Samantha is lost behind the reactions of the dynamic duo.

How do we free Samantha? First, we must write down all of her protective behaviors. Samantha initially sought counseling because she was unhappy with her stripping lifestyle. To free Samantha, we must deal not only with stripping but also with all of her protective behaviors. Second, we must connect the Protector to her motivating belief systems. Third, we must allow Samantha to tell us what her True Self believes. This process is called *dissecting*. An example of Samantha's protecting behaviors follows:

- Stripping
- Acting out sexually
- Using alcohol
- Controlling behavior
- Smoking
- Dishonesty
- Video poker

Connecting the Protector Behaviors With Beliefs and Motivating Feelings

Behavior	Protector's Belief	Wounded Child's Belief	Motivating Feeling
Stripping	Good money	Men have all power	Anger/hurt
Acting out	Sex= Love	Sex got me attention	Loneliness
Using alcohol	Feels good	Mom used it	Pain
Controlling	I have power	I have no power	Powerless/helpless
Smoking	Gives relief	I want to die	Hurt/betrayed
Dishonest	Tell them anything	I must survive	Terror/fear
Video poker	I will be rich	I'm poor	Shame

Next, we ask Samantha about Sugar's experiences that caused these beliefs. Samantha needs to do some grief work around the answers to these questions. At this point, Samantha needs to start an art and written journal.

Samantha's Wounded Child and Protector

Samantha needs to have her Wounded Child, Sugar, start to share about her beliefs and the experiences that caused the beliefs. She also needs to write about her feelings. Then she needs to let her Protector, Dancing Magnolia, talk about her beliefs and her feelings. Next, Samantha needs to parent, love, and nurture them. An example follows.

Sugar: I am scared. I don't like men, especially my stepfather. He did some very mean things to me. I want to die. Help me, help me. I'm scared. Nobody ever listens to me. I just keep quiet and don't talk. I'm real lonely. I like to hide in my closet because nobody could find me there, even my stepdad.

Dancing Magnolia: I love to be in control. If I'm in control, I can keep people at whatever distance I want to. I hate men. I love to tease them then reject the bastards. This writing stuff is so damn stupid.

Samantha: Sugar, I understand why you are so scared. Stepdad did some awful things. I am sorry you went through such horrible experiences. I love you, and I won't leave you anymore. Dancing Magnolia, I'm in control now. There will be no more dancing. I know you are very angry, yet it is not okay to hurt men anymore. These men are not stepfather. I have taken my body back. I want to hear what you have to say, but you cannot have my body.

In the beginning of dissection, the Wounded Child will talk only a little bit. This part holds all memory of the painful past, but it will withhold information until it is internally and externally safe enough. We must remember the Protector saved the individual's life; however, in the process, it traumatized the True Self and the Wounded Child. The internal trust level has been damaged severely. We must be persistent and enduring when building a relationship within. As the trust level is established, the memory will slowly return. Every time you remember a negative experience, you will also remember a positive one.

The dissecting process is the way to begin separating the three voices. All of our thoughts, behaviors, feelings, and reactions can be categorized in one of the voices. If we do not separate, we don't grow up. Life is lived either in the Protector or the Wounded Child. The Protector is the defensive, people-pleaser and the Wounded Child is the needy victim. Becoming a healthy adult means a person knows the internal belief systems and is able to live out of the True Self.

The belief system is the most important aspect of therapy. In some therapeutic approaches, the goal is to change the belief systems. The belief system of the Wounded Child and the Protector *cannot* be changed. The Wounded Child's belief system is completed by the age of ten, while the Protector's belief system is crystallized by age twenty. These beliefs are reinforced by life experiences. These systems are like two files in a computer that can never be erased. The only belief system that can change is the True Self. With time, maturity, and life experience, it will change the way it sees life. The thoughts of the Wounded Child and Protector, however, will always whisper or scream.

In Samantha's case, parts of her will always believe men will hurt her and must be kept away, while another part will desire the company of men friends. This internal struggle will continue throughout Samantha's life. The fight will decrease as Samantha understands the relationship between the voices. As a result, she will have the freedom to choose instead of reacting to her voices. As an adult woman, she can choose with whom she wants to be in a relationship and maintain the appropriate boundaries.

CHAPTER 9

Managing the Voices

The Lifelong Process

I Will Hold You

I know that life hasn't always been easy.
I remember the day the teacher broke her rules,
And hurt your little soul.
Innocence lost forever, and replaced by fear.

Today you know, I'm here for you
To embrace you forever more
When you are scared, you can talk to me.
And I will hold you in my arms.

I know that life hasn't always been easy.
I remember the day you were released,
released from the baseball team.
Failure felt deep in your soul and
want to cry in mama's arms.

Today you know, I'm here for you,
To embrace you forever more
When you are scared, you can talk to me.
And I will hold you in my arms.

I know that life hasn't always been easy.
I remember the day the puppy was hit,
by a speeding car.
He stopped breathing in your arms, and gone forever.

Today you know, I'm here for you,
To embrace you forever more.
When you are scared, you can talk to me.
And I will hold you in my arms.

After we understand and name our Wounded Child and
Protector, we have the rest of our lives to manage and love
them. The goal is for the dynamic duo to become thoughts
and voices instead of behaviors and reactions. We cannot allow these two voices to possess our bodies without permission,
or the results are tragic.

Clients often think they can come to one retreat or un-
dergo therapy for a year, and they will be fixed. Working
with the voices is not an event; it is a lifelong process. The
Wounded Child and Protector will always be present. The
Wounded Child will never be totally healed. The intensity of
the wounds will decrease by doing grief work, yet there will

always be a scar. Possession by the Protector is a lifelong struggle. When one is angry, lonely, hungry, or tired, one is most vulnerable to Protector possession. Our roadmap is to give you the skills to embrace them. The skills to work with the voices are more important than a cure.

Journaling

The first step in managing the voices is to become aware of who is talking outwardly and inwardly. You can do this by stopping and listening to your internal dialogue. One way of listening is by writing in a journal.

Journaling is important because you externalize the internal dialogue, which makes it easier to identify the belief systems. It is a way of self-mirroring and self-validating. In journaling, you must allow each voice to have some time to talk. We encourage clients to use different color inks for the different voices. The True Self must speak back to the other two in a parenting conversation. By this communication, you begin to build internal trust.

One example is a man named Joe who is journaling with his Wounded Child Dutch Boy and Protector Buckskin. On a Monday, the day after Mother's Day, Joe was at work unable to concentrate because his stomach was in emotional turmoil. He didn't know what was going on, so he decided to journal during lunch.

Joe: How are you doing Dutch Boy?

Dutch Boy: I am very sad. Yesterday was Mother's Day and I really miss Mom. I wish she wasn't dead. I just want to stay home and cry.

Joe: I know you are very sad. Mom was very important to us. I will take care of you now.

Buckskin: I got an idea. Let's go hang out with the guys at the pool hall and drink some beer. We'll forget about this stuff fast.

Joe: No, Buckskin, it is not okay for us to go to the pool hall anymore. I know you are mad and you have a right to be mad. You loved Mom. I'm in control now. I will take care of you and Dutch Boy.

Most of the time when we are triggered, it is not safe to work with the pain. Work is not a safe place for Joe to have his grief. He needs to contain his feelings until he is in a safe place. He needs to set a time and place that evening to work with Dutch Boy and Buckskin. If Joe promises them time and space that evening, the dynamic duo will not try to possess his body at work.

When Joe comes home from work, he needs to have an emotionally safe place and allow for some possession time. He needs a place in his house where he can have some solitude. He needs to allow Dutch Boy to write and draw about how much he misses his mother. Since Dutch Boy needs to do some grief work, Joe must permit Dutch Boy to possess his body and cry. Joe needs to put a time limit on the possession of perhaps twenty minutes. Joe also needs to allow Buckskin time to possess his body. Buckskin will need to express his anger by writing and drawing; again, there should be a time limit of perhaps twenty minutes. Then Joe will take his body back, knowing his grief about his mother will last a long time. Joe will validate Buckskin and Dutch Boy's pain by parenting them in a loving manner. An example follows.

Joe: Dutch Boy, now that we are home and safe, you can tell me more about what is going on.

Dutch Boy: In grammar school, Mom use to fix me lunch everyday. I miss those lunches. She made me feel good. I miss her. Is she gone forever? I want to cry thinking about her. (Joe cries in his heart and a few tears drop.)

Joe's Protector and Wounded Child

Joe: Dutch Boy, I know you miss Mom and the things she did for you. Mom was very kind, making lunches everyday. I will take care of you today. It's okay to cry, and I am happy you were able to get some of your feelings out. I love you. This weekend I will rent a sad movie so you can get some more pain out and get some relief.

Buckskin: I hate women. They are good to me for a little while, then they leave me. I want to punch the wall. I am so mad, so angry. Life sucks. I get close to a woman, and she leaves me. It ain't worth it. That's why I stay distant and leave them before they leave me.

Joe: Buckskin, I know you are mad and angry. I understand you are mad because Mom died and left you. You lost someone you love very much. Anytime someone loses

73

something that is important to them, they have angry feelings. I am glad you are talking about how angry you are. I love you.

If Joe does not deal with his pain, he will either carry it internally or he will act it out. *When the voices remain unconscious, the inner situation will appear outside as fate.* We will recreate our past hurts if we don't externalize them.

Writing and Drawing

We teach clients to manage their voices by writing and drawing. We found at times when we give a written homework assignment dealing with the Wounded Child, some of our clients can't do them. We realized the pre-verbal stage of the woundedness is so old they can't write. We used artwork, and these clients had been able to complete the assignments and get relief. The combination of keeping a written journal and an art journal has been very effective in breaking the bondage of the dynamic duo. Writing and drawing are two simple techniques, and they work.

Each of us needs to develop *inner ears*. We need to hear the voices. We need to listen to the thoughts, feelings, and beliefs of our Wounded Child and our Protector. We cannot embrace it unless we can hear it.

Given the Wounded Child has no sense of time and thinks symbolically, it is important to connect emotions with specific events. For example, Don is scared to talk in front of a group. His Wounded Child is carrying fear and terror due to an experience in fourth grade when he was forced to read in front of the class. He was not able to read because he was dyslexic, and the teacher made fun of him along with the class. Whenever Don gets up in front of a group as an adult, the fear and terror return.

In therapy, Don made the connection between this experience in fourth grade and his difficulty talking in front of a group. Don had his Wounded Child, Dopey, write about the fourth-grade incident and also do some grief work. Dopey believes he is stupid. His Protector, Shut Down, wouldn't let him talk in public. After connecting the incident with his fear and terror and the belief he is stupid, Don was able to separate from Dopey and Shut Down. He parented them by working with his voices in our retreat weekend, journaling, and group therapy. Don, the True Self, knows he is not stupid and is capable of speaking in a group. He recently was able to talk in front of a group at a business meeting with confidence.

Knowing Triggers

After we get to know our Wounded Child, we become sensitive to its triggers. Part of managing the voices is to know what are our triggers. It is inevitable we will be triggered; the key is to know what to do when it happens. Some of HollyKem's triggers are male authority figures, angry people, loudness, being ignored, and feeling controlled. She knows if any of these happen, she will be filled with a high intensity of emotion. Her Wounded Child or Protector will try to possess her. She will need to figure out who is talking and calm this part of her.

We need to understand the behaviors of our Protector. Our Protector may have a desire to drink, clean compulsively, shop, work, eat, starve, act out sexually, or "fix" someone. When we have a strong urge to act out with these behaviors, it is a sign something is going on with the Wounded Child. The behaviors always connect to our woundedness.

Exercise

Go back to the questions on the Protector and the Wounded Child. List the major wounds you experienced in column A. In column B, list your protective behaviors.

The purpose of this exercise is to help you figure out when you are possessed. This information is like an alarm system. When it is set off, you need to take action and work with your Protector and Wounded Child instead of them working you. We suggest you read this list many times and memorize the information.

Managing the Voice of the True Self

Just as we must know the Protector and the Wounded Child, we must also know the True Self. When the True Self emerges, it has a lot to say. There must be a safe avenue for this part to speak, because this voice is often ridiculed and shut down by other people's Protectors. This part is shut down by our Protector! The True Self needs an unlimited source of expression. Writing and artwork is an excellent way to let the soul shine.

This is where your vision is very important. Your hopes, dreams, desires, and passions are implanted in your True Self, and it must be given a chance to blossom. Listen to your soul. This is where the magic is. Your *field of dreams* is waiting to be unlocked. It is not about fame and fortune but about finding your convictions and living by them with courage, trust, and hope. It is *being* in your body not just doing.

Affirmations

We have confidence you will spontaneously find your vision and passion after you have separated from the Wounded Child and Protector. How do you make your vision become a reality? One powerful way is to nurture your vision through affirmation work. This means you constantly remind yourself of the vision through writing. The imagination is greater than the will. If the imagination is persistent in its vision, it will eventually convert the will. For example, if you want to be a healthy communicator in your relationships, you can use this affirmation:Thank you, God, for making me a healthy communicator in all my relationships.

We had a male client who went through our weekend retreat program and worked very hard on his voices within. After leaving an abusive marriage of ten years, he began to repeat this affirmation: Thank You, God, for my healthy marriage.

He met a healthy, loving woman and was married. The woman said to him she had waited her whole life for him. He worked on himself, made a vision, nurtured it with affirmations, and trusted in God. The results are miraculous!

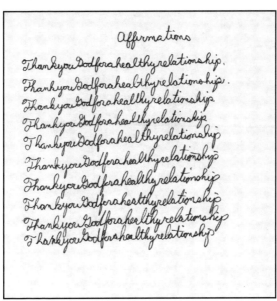

Affirmations without lifting the pen.

In writing affirmations, we recommend two rules. First, write the same affirmation ten times a day. Second, do not lift your pen or pencil when writing the sentence. Write in script and connect all the words. By connecting all of the words, the thought remains connected in the mind. We have witnessed some phenomenal changes in our lives and in people who have done this type of affirmation.

Images

For people who are vision oriented, affirmation work can be done by way of images. By creating visual images, such as pictures and collages, you can affirm daily your vision by seeing yourself in these pictures. For example, on our refrigerator we have a photograph of the house in which we want to live. We see this picture daily and we imagine ourselves in this home. This home is a southern plantation, and we dream of transforming the plantation into a retreat center. We constantly nurture this vision on a daily basis, and we believe one day we will be in the plantation.

A collage is a visual image created by getting some old magazines and a poster board. Look through the magazines

Example of a Collage.

and cut out images or words regarding a certain subject that appeal to you. The subject could be a future family, a dream home, an ideal job, and so forth. After you gather the words and images, you glue them onto the poster board. This collage provides a nice image that affirms your True Self vision daily.

Peace of Mind

The purpose of working with the voices and managing them is to find and keep a quietness in the mind and heart. Serenity has been the quest for humans in many of the great spiritual traditions including our Judeo-Christian tradition. Serenity is a result of listening to the True Self and activating its vision. If we are lost in the clamor of the Wounded Child and Protector, we never get to a quiet place of listening. Energy is focused on escaping the clamor, leaving the body, and dissociating from the echoing emptiness—*the internal black hole*. Inwardly, we hear the screams of the voices but we also find the place of peace. It is the sacred ground of the soul. After we taste its delights of contentment, it gives us the courage to carry on. Finding the voice of the True Self and responding to its inspiration are the only ways to find lasting peace.

CHAPTER 10

Couple-ship

Coupleship is a significant relationship between two people and the commitment may vary from socially close friends to a married couple. Coupleship is a wonderful adventure that will challenge us to grow more than any other relationship. But why is coupleship so difficult? Why do half of the marriages in the United States end in divorce? Why do some couples that stay together end up bitter and unhappy? This is a million-dollar question.

The people closest to us trigger our Wounded Child. In a strange way, that is their job. Our wounds are what keeps us distant and isolated from other people. If our partner triggers our wounds, they have a chance to come to the surface and to experience some healing. Couples and marriages are destroyed because the individual does not know how to embrace his or her *own wounds*. Hence, their Protector reacts and does something he or she later regrets.

Here are some examples:

- John is hurt by his wife, so he acts out sexually.
- Cathy is afraid to be home at night alone, so she drinks her fear away.
- Mark is angry about his wife's complaining, so he works overtime to avoid her.
- Maria is angry because her husband won't listen, so she has an affair.

An Internal Journey

The biggest mistake couples make in therapy is they focus on the relationship and neglect the internal journey inside themselves. Couples counseling works when each person makes a commitment to work on him- or herself rather than the relationship. If a person does not know his or her history or has protectively blocked it out, it is impossible to communicate who he or she is to another person. History–his- or her-story–needs to be known and embraced. It is much easier to focus on the faults and shortcomings of a partner than it is to embrace one's *his-story*.

In our language, the Protector will block one's history because it may trigger pain. Yet, the purpose of a relationship is to trigger each other's history so it can come to the surface. When our wounds are brought to the surface, healing may occur. Our wounds keep us from loving ourselves, other people, and God. If these wounds have a chance to heal, then we grow in these three relationships. If we don't have the skills to help us heal, we play these wounds out on each other. *This is not fun!*

Mary argued frequently with her husband Tom because he worked late on a Friday night. This was the first time Tom needed to work late in years. It was a project that needed to be completed by Saturday. She acted as if Tom stayed out on Friday and had an affair with another woman. At this juncture, one or two things could happen. Mary would rant and rave, accusing Tom of having an affair. He would deny it and tell her how ridiculous she was behaving. They would argue and scream for a few hours, then move into silence, perhaps for two days. The issue would probably not be resolved, and it would become another scar in their history together.

The second way this scenario could work out is that Mary could tell Tom when he got home that a part of her (the Wounded Child) was scared he was having an affair. She would explain when she was a little girl, her father would stay out on Friday night and she heard he cheated on her mother. She remembers her mother screaming at her father when he got home on Friday night. Mary could explain to Tom she is transferring her hurt and anger about her father having affairs onto Tom. He would be able to listen and understand the intensity of her feelings because she could connect it with her history. The conversation would become a moment of *intimacy* instead of *isolation*.

The difference between the two scenarios is whether or not Mary knew and understood her unique history. If she denied her history, the incident would have erupted into a fight. The solution was not to fix Tom but to work internally. By understanding her voices within (the Wounded Child, "scared of an affair," and the Protector, "wanting to rant and rave"), she can connect triggers to her history and communicate this. Intimacy is the result.

Listening

Listening is the act of being open to hearing what another is saying, and it requires great effort and concentration. Listening is 90 percent of communication. Often, when someone is talking to us, we are thinking about a response or about something else. This is a classic Protector behavior that blocks connection. Group therapy is a very powerful experience when members of the group can listen to each other. When this occurs, the healing exchange that follows is beyond words.

Listening is also the greatest tool in a successful relationship. For example, HollyKem has felt lonely most of her life. One day she realized she never felt lonely after a session as a therapist. It dawned on her this was because she had listened and understood her client to the best of her ability. The simple–yet difficult–act of listening was all it took to help another person feel loved. HollyKem began doing this with friends, family, and her boyfriend, who today is her husband. Her loneliness problem has been solved. If she feels isolated or lonely, she calls a friend or talks to her husband and asks how he or she is doing.

Four Loves

In a couple, it is important to figure out what type of love the relationship is based. In the Greek language, there are four different words for love: *philia, storge, eros,* and *agape. Philia* is used as a root for the word Philadelphia, the city of brotherly love. It literally means "friendship love." It is characterized by an equivalence in the relationship that includes an equality in power. *Philia* is the type of love you have with a best friend. It is nonpossessive, free, and life-giving to both people. The ancient Greeks regarded *philia* as the most important type of love. They believed if you had much friendship love in your life, you would be happy.

84

Storge is translated as parental love. It is a one-sided love of giving without expecting too much in return. *Storge* is the type of love a parent has for a child. The balance of power is unequal, because one person has most of the power while the other is powerless.

Eros is the root word for erotic. It translates into English as sexual love. *Eros* is a highly energized type of love that characterizes a romantic relationship in its early stages. It can be overpowering and is associated with passion, creativity, and vibrancy.

Agape is a word invented in early Christian times that describes God's love for His people. It is also known as unconditional love, a high spiritual state that is the ideal for human relationships. It takes much hard work and spiritual discipline to achieve this state of relating. Unconditional love is the foundation for healing, human growth, and fulfillment.

The type of love that dominates the couple relationship is very important. A relationship based on *philia* or friendship love usually lasts and is fulfilling. A couple that has much of this energy enjoys being together, won't be possessive, and can negotiate conflict as equals.

If the individuals in a relationship are possessed often by their Wounded Child or Protector, their relating is characterized by much *storge* or parental love. One person dominates while the other feels powerless. This balance of power will shift according to the topic of conversation. Games of power, control, and possessiveness are constantly played. A Protector addresses the other person's Wounded Child: "You can never make it without me, because you can't financially take care of yourself." "I can't live alone, the thought is terrifying," whispers the Wounded Child. This type of relationship causes resentment in both partners, because one is forced into a parental role while the other is being treated as a child. Both people are unhappy, but it is safer than being abandoned or left on one's own.

A relationship that is based on *eros* or erotic love has a quick start. It may last a couple of months to a couple of years. A couple that gets married with only this energy may have good sex, but they probably don't enjoy being together in social situations. *Eros* is an overpowering type of love, and the people who use this to deny their feelings compulsively act out sexually.

Agape is the ideal for a relationship, but this type of love can only be achieved after totally embracing the Wounded Child and containing the Protector. It is a gift given to people who are connected intimately with their God. *Agape* is the foundation for miracles, empowerment, self-esteem, and life-giving creativity.

In a relationship, it is normal to have a combination of these different types of love. In general, couples who are having difficulty need to work on increasing the *philia* or friendship. If *philia* is the firm foundation, *eros* can come and go and the relationship will last. If the couple has a lot of *storge*, or parental love, each person needs to do much work to revive the relationship. Embracing their own Voices Within is the only hope of reviving the relationship.

Intimacy

Intimacy is knowing oneself and one's feelings and thoughts, and communicating these to another. Fear of intimacy is based on being wounded. Because one of the purposes of a relationship is to trigger our Wounded Child, the fear of intimacy is the fear of having our Wounded Child exposed. What will happen if my internalized pain comes to the surface? "I'll be totally overwhelmed." "I might not survive." "Letting go is terrifying." These are some of the answers we have heard in our practice. Yes, it is a risk and it is also the doorway to our soul. Our internalized pain keeps us from the sunlight of our soul.

How can a relationship be revived? The greatest contribution an individual can make in improving a relationship is to work on him- or herself. This means identifying and understanding one's Protector and Wounded Child. It is your responsibility to take care of your own Wounded Child, not your partner's. It is your responsibility to separate the past from the present and to listen and communicate your wants, needs, dreams, and desires. Be committed to finding your True Self and the relationship will work out as it needs to.

Intimacy

Is knowing me to the fullest.
Trusting Me–Risking Me
Loving Me–Changing Me, which needs changing
And–most of all, taking responsibility for
My Wounded Child
My Protector
and
My True Self
Emotionally, Spiritually, Physically and Mentally
So I'm not lonely.

Spirituality

CHAPTER 11

What Is Spirituality?
Addicted Religion

Lost in religion of fear and hate,
Fundamentally above the rest of the race.
Trying to escape this evil human body,
Can't get to Easter, cause I'm stuck in Good Friday.

Wake Up from the trance
God doesn't live in the clouds.
Stand up before Him, and shout out loud.
Pray with the passion of Job,
Who found peace in his rage at God,
Embraced his Pain and was Reborn into Life.

Entrenched in beliefs that give security,
Trying to save Souls with Righteous purity.
Fighting the Spirit from getting too close,
Damaging lives, using the Lord of Host.

Wake Up from the trance
God doesn't live in the clouds.
Stand up before Him, and shout out loud.
Pray with the passion of Job,
Who found peace in his rage at God,
Embraced his Pain and was Reborn into Life.

Judging the world with Myopic Eyes
The Heart is lost behind Stormy Skies.
Living Alone in Cerebral tendencies,
Creating a hell, using Christianity.

Wake Up from the trance
God doesn't live in the clouds.
Stand up before Him, and shout out loud.
Pray with the passion of Job,
Who found peace in his rage at God,
Embraced his Pain and was Reborn into Life.

Human inadequacy ruling the soul.
Addicted Religion can't fill the Hole.
Buried in shame, turned false humility.
Without fighting the interior Enemy.

Wake Up from the trance
God doesn't live in the clouds.
Stand up before Him, and shout out loud.

Pray with the passion of Job,
Who found peace in his rage at God,
Embraced his Pain and was Reborn into Life.

This chapter is perhaps the most important in the entire book. Spirituality is where our humanity ends and God begins. This boundary is often unclear in today's society. Some people emphasize the importance of humanity and neglect the role of a creator (atheism and agnosticism), while others disregard our humanity in the midst of a religious escapism (religious addiction). Before we tackle this problem, we must first understand our idea of God from the perspective of the Voices Within. The following exercise will help you to clarify your vision of God, religion, and spirituality.

Exercise

1. As a child, what was your religion and your perception of God? If you did not have a religion, what was the most important ideal in your family?

2. As a teenager and young adult, did you accept or reject the answer to question 1? Explain.

3. What are your present beliefs about religion, God, and spirituality?

The three most important relationships we have as human beings are those with God, our fellow human beings, and ourselves. In the Jewish, Moslem, and Christian traditions, the foundational commandment is to love the Lord your *God* with all your heart, soul, and mind and to love your *neighbor* as *yourself*. Spirituality is the quality of these three relationships. If a person has a deep love of oneself and is able to reach out and love others and is open to the communion with their God, this individual is spiritual.

Spirituality is a simple concept, but we make it complicated with complex theological ideas. One of the greatest people Dean ever met was a priest named Francis Harpin. He was a brilliant yet simple man who had a tremendous capacity to accept people unconditionally. He had a deep love and acceptance of his human condition, knowing clearly his gifts and his shortcomings. Dean had the privilege of living with him for three months in Italy; Dean was amazed at how people responded to him. From Cardinals in the Catholic Church to the maintenance man at the basilica, they opened their hearts to his healing, unconditional love. He was able to relate to Christians, Jews, Buddhists, and Moslems in a way that transcended the bounds of their religions. He also spent time each day meditating and working on his relationship with God. It was not a highly spiritual thing, but a real, human, and simple trust in God. He was truly a spiritual man. He taught Dean a prayer that is perfect for helping with spiritual growth; he still says each morning:

God grant me a deeper knowledge and love of You,
a deeper knowledge and love of myself,
and a deeper knowledge and love of
every individual that I meet today.

* * * * *

Good and evil are two terms used often in theology. A simple definition is that good is whatever helps to improve these three relationships, whereas evil is anything that destroys these relationships. For example, a walk in the park, coffee with a friend, and quiet meditation time are good activities. Abusing the body with food, raging at children, or not making time to pray to God are destructive activities.

Difference Between Religion and Spirituality

Since spirituality measures the quality of relationships with God, the self, and other people, religion is the institution that was built to nurture these three associations. Some religious institutions have lost the vision of spirituality and no longer feed their congregation. The survival of the institution has become more important than the human spirit. Obligation and fear motivate the congregation rather than love and a thirst for God. A congregation can be a wonderful institution when it feeds the spirit of people, and this is translated into daily life. Yet, when religions are promoting fear, separation, righteousness and hatred, they need to be challenged.

When involvement in religion is motivated by the True Self, it is an awesome experience. When involvement is motivated by the Protector, it becomes a way to escape our human condition. It is a way to spiritualize our pain, thoughts, and actions while we seek a life outside our human bodies. Religious addiction is the result. Scripture, orthodoxy, and teachings become an avenue for denying anger, sadness, and loneliness. Instead of embracing our human condition of joy and pain, the Protector religion stops the flow of feeling.

When religious participation is motivated by the Wounded Child, an immature faith is the result. Fear of God motivates the individual, and beliefs are black and white with no room for any gray area. Strict obedience to authority and unquestioned teachings keep individuals enslaved to their fear.

If religious involvement is motivated by the True Self, the person grows in the three relationships. Religion becomes a means to discover purpose, passion, creativity, courage, and hope. It helps one embrace and understand our human condition.

Some general characteristics of religion and spirituality include the following:

Spirituality	Religion
Individual	Communal
Internal Authority	External Authority
Experience	Tradition
Emotional	Intellectual
Personal	Group

Three Levels of Belief

In terms of a relationship with God, there are three possible levels of believing: atheist, agnostic, and personal relationship. An atheist is someone who believes there is no God and is usually stuck in their Protector voice. Because we are human, this person has an ultimate belief system, but it is not God. Where does he or she put their power? Work, money, sex, intellect, institutions, and drugs are a few examples of false dependencies. We are made to be connected soulfully with God. Codependency is when we are overly connected with created things, and our souls are restless until they find God. Some atheists say they don't believe in anything. This is probably not true. Their god is what is most important in their life.

An agnostic is a person who believes there is a God but God is not involved in his or her life. The agnostic is a doubter and needs proof. Unfortunately, true faith is based on an experience that comes after a leap of faith. Many agnostics feel they are not worthy of God's love and abundance because of their history. This keeps them a safe distance from their Creator. They are stuck in the Wounded Child voice.

The personal relationship is characterized by an authentic connection with the Creator. This person takes the leap of faith and has the ability to trust as a child trusts a loving parent. This individual knows that regardless of life events and circumstances, God will not abandon. This is the foundation for living peacefully inside our bodies.

The Second Conversion

The second conversion is another way of describing the emergence of the soul. We develop our first belief system as children by accepting the beliefs of our parents, schools, friends, and religion. This belief system is also based on the wounds that are experienced in childhood. Our first conversion occurs during the development of our Protector, and it is either the total acceptance or total rejection of the first belief system. If you think it sounds like adolescence, you are right. Many people stay stuck in the first conversion and live their lives this way.

The opportunities for the second conversion occur throughout adulthood. God gives us many occasions to move to the second conversion. Each of these events is a crisis that provides the opportunity to stop and reflect on our lives. The middle-aged man dealing with the death of his best friend suddenly finds himself reflecting on childhood, mortality, purpose, his marriage, and career. At this juncture, he can either embrace his life and pain, or he can let his Protector take off and run.

The crisis is like an earthquake that destroys the structure of the Wounded Child and the Protector. It provides the opportunity for the True Self to break through. The individual may awaken or go back to sleep. If one stays awake, he or she will hear the voice of the True Self. Because of the fear of embracing one's pain (the Wounded Child) and one's defense mechanisms (the Protector), some choose to stay stuck in soul-less living. Midlife crisis, death, addiction, divorce, accidents, and disease are all opportunities to move into the second conversion.

The second conversion is finding and living by the beliefs of the True Self. This belief system emerges when we separate the Wounded Child and the Protector. We must challenge our own belief system with love. One may choose to keep or change their childhood and adolescent belief system, yet the challenge is crucial. The object of the Voices Within is not to change the belief system of the Wounded Child and the Protector, but it is to know the difference between the True Self, the Protector, and the Wounded Child. Our goal in life is to live by the voice of the True Self. This is freedom. This is soulful living. This is the Promise Land.

True Self and God

Working with the Voices Within is a journey to the True Self or Soul. The True Self is the crossroad where we meet our God, our vision, our creativity, peace of mind, and love. After separating our Wounded Child and Protector, the voice of the True Self emerges.

People often ask what is God's will for me? God's will and the vision of our True Self are the same. Our soul's dreams are not different from the will of God. When one is in touch with their soul, a person knows in which direction they must travel because the soul will speak to them and God will open the doors. We tell our clients to just start walking toward their dreams and watch God do miracles.

You are and become what you believe. If your God is small, your harvest will be small. If your God is tremendous, your harvest will be tremendous. The greatest challenge we have as people is simply accepting the abundance that God is capable of giving us. It is easier to not challenge our beliefs and settle for a small God than it is go on the adventure of embracing a God of huge proportions. Look into the mirror and say five times a day, "God loves me." Say it as if you believe it.

A coincidence or synchronicity is a common event when we begin to walk toward the vision of our True Self. A man who wants to develop his musical talent suddenly meets a music teacher. A woman who recently quit a job she is unhappy in gets a lead on a job in the field she has been dreaming about. These events happen all the time. It is as if the universe is becoming a partner in delivering our vision. Be open; accept and trust. If one stops blocking it, God's power can produce the miracles.

Therapy
Only God Can Heal the Broken Heart

Make it safe, so hurt can talk,
Takes away fear, what a great start.
Love the Wound, see a fragile heart,
Turn to God to heal the broken part

Only God can heal the damaged soul
Many try but they just don't know.
Human nature can go so far,
Only God can heal the broken Heart.

Awareness of life, professionals say,
Makes the journey in life a happy stay.
Uncover the burdens that drive the thoughts,
Yet turn to God to heal the broken part.

Only God can heal the damaged soul
Many try but they just don't know.
Human nature can go so far,
Only God can heal the broken Heart.

Release emotion in therapy,
At an impasse, stuck energy.
Feelings released, exhausted soul,
Turn to God to heal the weary soul.

Only God can heal the damaged soul
Many try but they just don't know.
Human nature can go so far,
Only God can heal the broken Heart.

Change your thoughts, Uncle Albert would say,
Bad thoughts make a miserable day.
Forget emotions, silly human part,
Turn to God to heal the broken part.

Only God can heal the damaged soul
Many try but they just don't know.
Human nature can go so far,
Only God can heal the broken Heart.

Therapy is a process of healing. The word therapy comes from the Greek root that means *to heal.* As counselors, we are simply the channels or instruments of healing. God is the one who does the healing. Our wounds have the potential to be healed to the extent they no longer control our lives and decisions. They are never healed completely. Healing means being loved in pain. First another loves us, then we learn to love ourselves. We call this process embracing our Wounded

Child and Protector. Our clients who invite God to be a part of their process of healing move much faster than the clients who do not. An individual may do a tremendous amount of work in therapy, releasing emotion, containing thoughts, solving problems; nevertheless, if they don't develop a relationship with God, deep anxiety will continue. When the True Self uncovers its God, peace can finally invade the body. Nothing in the world can shake this foundation—not even death.

The twelve-step movement is perhaps the most powerful spiritual movement of the twentieth century. The twelve steps are a tool that can be used to uncover the True Self and God. They are designed to create a greater love and acceptance of oneself, to amend past relationships, and to awaken to a new perception of God. The steps represent spirituality at its finest. We support the twelve-step programs in all their different forms.

The spiritual journey is recovery. Recover the lost self. The True Self is there, waiting to be liberated from the layers of pain and protective defenses. The Voices Within is a roadmap to the soul.

CHAPTER 12

Conclusion

Emotional and Spiritual Freedom

The journey described in this book is one of many ways to find your soul. We have experienced in our own lives and seen in the lives of many others miraculous results. The journey inward is risky, vulnerable, painful, and scary, but at the same time freeing, peaceful, soulful, and real. We challenge you to take the risk—embrace your Wounded Child and love your Protector. Open your ears to the voice of your soul so you can live in the Promise Land.

You have the right to live soulfully where there are no clouds and the heat of love keeps you warm twenty-four hours a day. It is a place where you see things clearly and free of all frustration, hatred, and mistrust. You are pure, authentic, and free–free to embrace your passion, to play spontaneously, and to give and accept love without condition or limit. Free to dream, chase dreams and even achieve them. The soul is a safe place where devastation and past wounds do not possess the present and self-destructive behavior is bridled and controlled. A place in the soul is warm, tender, and smoothly proportioned as one looks into the mirror. "I am good" is the echo that rings from one's soul and absorbed into the many fibers of the body. Living in the soul is seeing clearly, the past and present are joined in a puzzle that makes sense, and makes me have self-compassion and self-love. The soul is a place to have the passionate, creative voice that howls, crying with excitement, "I Have A Voice."

See you in the Promise Land!

Soulfully,

HollyKem

Dean

HollyKem and Dean Sunseri are leaders of a small team of therapist who have helped many individuals achieve physical, emotional and spiritual wellness. HollyKem and Dean created a retreat model that has been transformational. By combining education, creative expression with a safe atmosphere, this unique experience has helped revive relationships, relieve depression, provide recovery from addiction and relieve emotional pain. The retreat is also a wellness model that facilitates creativity, empowers dreams, builds a healthy spirituality and promotes soulful living.

Our Life Enrichment Retreats take place at Jolimar Summit Wellness Institute, a beautiful Holistic Health Club on 890 acres outside of Summit, Mississippi. All of our different retreat programs integrate The Voices Within concept.

The different programs are:

Original Retreatment

Our Original Retreatment program helps individuals grow psychologically, emotionally and spiritually. Using The Voices Within, we provide participants a safe, supportive atmosphere where they may address self-destructive behaviors that prevent soulful living. We help people recover from relationship issues, multiple addictions, codependency and family of origin issues.

Our program, which teaches communication skills, boundary setting and self-respect, gives each person a Roadmap to their own Soul.

Family Matters

Family matters is a special Retreatment Program for families. It has two primary objectives. First, we provide individuals a safe, supportive atmosphere where they may recover their True Self. Second, we provide a forum for family members to create healthier relationships with each other.

While doing individual work in a group setting with other family members present, powerful transformations take place. As each person begins to share, they often release years of barriers in minutes as intolerance and resentments are replaced by love, honor and respect. The result is a new basis for future relationships between family members.

Beyond Diets

Beyond Diets is a comprehensive process for people who suffer from an unhealthy relationship with food and struggle with a negative body image. Our program is especially helpful to those who suffer from overeating, bulimia and anorexia.

To have a healthy relationship with food, people must work with the emotional, mental and spiritual issues, as well as physical attachments. We attribute the success of our program to the fact that we address each of these areas. We help our clients build a bridge between unhealthy behaviors with food and the underlying causes.

Kid Talk

Children have strong emotional and developmental needs that need considerable nurturing. Due to the emotional challenges of growing up, they sometimes begin to exert self-defeating behaviors such as low self-esteem, depression, addiction, sexual acting out and anger problems.

Our program, derived from The Voices Within concept, teaches children how to love themselves and begin taking care of themselves. We offer a forum for them to safely experience and release their pain. The program includes education, art therapy, group therapy and communication games.

Intensive Individual Retreatment

Our Intensive Individual Retreatment Program offers all of the benefits of our Original Retreatment Program but is conducted on an individual basis instead of in a group setting.

In a one-on-one process with one of our trained professionals, participants are allowed considerable time to work on relationship issues, multiple addictions, codependency and family of origin issues.

Our goal is to give the program participant his own Roadmap to the Soul.

Our **New Perspectives Program** is a 14-day program that promotes a healthy relationship with food. This eating wellness program has helped individuals who struggle with overeating, binging, purging, and starvation. By addressing the underlying causes of unhealthy eating , body image issues, we help our clients move to a new level of freedom.

For the dates and times for the upcoming retreats, you can call HollyKem and Dean's office, **Evergreen Wellness Center at 1-888-889-7600** or you can call **Jolimar Summit Wellness Institute at 1-800-243-3993.**

Seminars, Workshops, Consultations

HollyKem and Dean have translated their message to help and inspire individuals in many different settings. Their workshops and seminars have empowered small businesses to large corporation, and their message has inspired groups at banquets, conventions and churches. If you are interested in setting up a speaking engagement, you can contact them toll-free at 1-888-889-7600 or www.IHaveAVoice.com.

Give the Gift of

A Roadmap to the Soul

to Your Friends and Colleagues

CHECK YOUR LEADING BOOKSTORE OR ORDER HERE

❑ **YES**, I want ___ copies of *A Roadmap to the Soul* at $16.95 each, plus $3 shipping per book (Louisiana residents please add .68 sales tax per book). Canadian orders must be accompanied by a postal money order in U.S. funds. Allow 15 days for delivery.

(See other side for Audio Tapes available from TVW Publishing)

My check or money order for $_____ is enclosed.

Please charge my ❑ Visa ❑ MasterCard

Name _____

Organization _____

Address _____

City/State/Zip _____

Phone _____ E-mail _____

Card # _____ Exp. Date _____

Signature _____

Please make your check payable and return to:

TVW Publishing

3017 12th Street, Metairie, LA 70002

Call your credit card order to:
(504) 838-0486 or (888)-889-7600
Fax: (504) 838-0156
www.IHaveAVoice.com

Audio Tapes

Quantity		
☐	A Roadmap to the Soul (4 cassette series) HollyKem and Dean Sunseri	$29.95
☐	The Voices Within and the 12 Steps HollyKem and Dean Sunseri	$10.00
☐	Redefining Spirituality Dean Sunseri	$10.00
☐	Parenting: Maintaining Emotional Health HollyKem Sunseri	$10.00
☐	Creating Intimacy in a Relationship HollyKem and Dean Sunseri	$10.00
☐	Creating Love HollyKem Sunseri	$10.00
☐	Developing Your Creativity Dean Sunseri	$10.00
☐	Songs for the Soul - Music on CD Written & Sung by Dean Sunseri	$10.00
☐	Songs for the Soul - Music Tape Written & Sung by Dean Sunseri	$ 8.00

Add $3.00 Shipping & Handling per order please

(**Fill out payment and shipping information on other side**)

Mail or fax to:

TVW Publishing

3017 12th Street, Metairie, LA 70002

(504) 838-0486 or 888-889-7600

Fax (504) 838-0156

www.IHaveAVoice.com